Ira Joe Fisher

IRA JOE FISHER

Wide and Wavy Out of Salamanca

Sort of True Essays

November 5, 2020

For Ted and Susan ···

Some musings
that I hope you enjoy.
Merriness to you and ···

··· love,

Ira

{ A }
Athanata
ARTS LTD.

"I'LL BE HOME FOR CHRISTMAS"

by Walter Kent, Kim Gannon & Buck Ram

Copyright © 1943 (Renewed 1971) by Gannon & Kent Music (ASCAP)

International Copyright Secured. All Rights Reserved. Used by Permission.

"NOBODY CARES ABOUT THE RAILROADS ANYMORE"

Words and Music by HARRY NILSSON

Copyright © 1969 (Renewed) GOLDEN SYRUP MUSIC

All Rights Administered by WARNER-TAMERLANE PUBLISHING CORP.

All Rights Reserved. Used By Permission of ALFRED MUSIC.

Library of Congress Control Number: 2020933552

First edition

ISBN: 978-0-9727993-9-3

This book was professionally typeset on Reedsy.
Find out more at reedsy.com

For Robert J. Miller, beloved "Boober." You graced Little Valley and me with brotherly love, kindness, laughing, smiling, plotting ... and enough mischief to keep our families', our teachers', and the sheriff's deputies' heads shaking. But above all, you graced Little Valley and me with ... grace. The grace of a loving friendship. From deep in childhood ... on into this century.

Contents

Preface

Read, Speak, Write

A book. All my life a book has sat upon my mind, weighed upon my hand like a moment to anticipate, like a chest whose treasure is sparkling light, a talisman. The first book I read cover to cover? *All for a Horse* by Kay Avery. In that book a little boy dreamed and wished and worked for his own horse. My dreams were always about dogs. Reading on, I went into the jungle where Tarzan was born and reared by apes (in a book my father gave to me from *his* childhood). A book. Each day something to look forward to. A book. Small in my pocket. Large in my heart. And always waiting at the end of the day to end the day with slow, sparkling, magic. The lilt of Frost and the wink of Dickinson; the heat o' Shakespeare and the grace of Lloyd C. Douglas; E. B. White's gentle, timid essaying and Daphne du Maurier's no-name mist on a Cornwall coast. Dickens. Maugham. Barrett Browning. Mary Oliver. They gave me a book. They gave me a reason to rise every morning. A book. Always there. Always here.

At the age of four I realized I wanted to entertain, to notice. And (I blush here) to *be* noticed. As a teenager I became a radio announcer. At the age of sixteen I spoke into a microphone and confirmed the notion I had that this is how I wanted to spend my life. The love led also to network television and the New York stage. And imbued me with a philosophy for expressing thought, sense, inspiration. How to subdue any trepidation before an audience ... large or little. How to communicate so as to make each member of the audience—*large or little*—feel singled out for what I have to say. It's a compelling philosophy, and I determined to apply it every day of my life. I reduce several things to one thing. I approach an audience of many as an audience of one. I speak. And I listen. Communicating isn't about uninterrupted noise. It's also about silence, the power of the pause. Drama. Soul. Rememberings. It is a great grace.

A door to that vast meadow called *imagination*. That's what I look for in life. The remembered thought, carried on the back of honored language, to the remembered end. From my years as a reporter and interviewer, as an actor and poet, I learned to pay attention to a question's answer, to respond to a person's comments and mood, to regard each *spontaneous* comment—or scripted line—as if it were being uttered for the first time. The student *teaches* as much as she *learns*. Each day brings a moment to notice, a lesson to teach, a lesson to learn. Some lessons ask us to speak. Some ask us to just listen. Then to breathe those lessons into sound. Or sense-making ink.

This book carries some of my thinkings. Serious and silly, shallow or an attempt at depth. It carries rememberings of friends and loves and faces. Many of the people and some of the dogs and all of the places still exist. Many are ghosts who still give me smiles and wisdom and shivers of grief.

It's no coincidence that *summer* and *swelter* and *sizzle* all begin with a sibilant S. It's the season. And why God invented air-conditioning and refrigerators and Fudgsicles. And catcher's mitts, village parks, vacations, lakes, Good Humor trucks, oak trees, leafy streets, and panting pups. Summer is why we open our windows at night. It's why wind whispers in the leaves and why shade invites us to sit. Summer. When thunderstorms grumble. And with all that rain, summer never cools. It's glowing days and firefly eves that always sigh, "Whew." But with a smile. Let's smile back. Here is a bundle of musings. From my bundle of years. I give you the bundle to read. Or throw away. But I give my bundle to *you*.

Acknowledgement

Some of these writings—or versions of them—first appeared in *Spokane Magazine*, *OfficeInsight*, and lectures at colleges and universities. My gratitude for consent to include them in this collection.

I

Soup and Song

Soda Jerk

"Professional Building." The words were carved into the granite lintel. *Professional Building.* Reassuring. I'd have hesitated to enter an amateur building. So enter I did. And I was whooshed back in time. Right into an old, sagging drugstore with a soda fountain. In the twenty-first century ... a soda fountain! I swear I heard laughter roiling the air from people named Emmie Lou and Boober; Harlow and Fern.

I was in a northern Vermont village. A late-morning lunch in this clean and ancient place seemed a great idea. I sat on a stool and asked for a cup of potato soup. As I waited, I looked around. There was a Coca-Cola machine—red and rounded with a here-and-there dent. On the wall behind it a handwritten sign announced, "5 cent Cokes are back: one per person, one per day." A bargain to be sure. And unambiguous. You want a nickel Coke? Fine. Just don't expect a second one. 'Til tomorrow.

Off in the small kitchen (from which wafted intimations of grilled cheese and "we only serve well-done" burgers) I spotted uncut loaves of just-baked bread in glinting plastic bags. They were so appealing they could almost restore a carb's good name.

As my soup vigil continued, my eye traveled to another sign on the wall: "New menus are out"—at first I thought this meant the new menus were *gone*, but I read on. "Be sure to check our newly added items." "New" and "newly" felt a tad forced in their cheery adjective and adverb insistence in so old-fashioned a setting.

I had a favorite book with me and I could have opened it while waiting, but there was more to ponder from the wall in this aged drugstore soda fountain. I swiveled my attention a few degrees to the ice cream sector. This boasted the obligatory and universal chocolate and vanilla. You could enjoy "cookies 'n cream," a flavor that troubled me because of its missing second apostrophe. Vermonters are usually so good at contractions. There was "butter crunch" and "rum raisin." But then I spotted the regional reasons we love New England: "deer tracks" and "moose tracks" and … "dinosaur crunch." Now, *those* are flavors!

Okay, I confess that my first glance alarmed me into reading "deer tracks" as "deer ticks" and the notion of Lyme disease zagged through my brain. "Moose tracks" brought me back to whimsical reality. There are moose everywhere in northern Vermont. Artistically, that is. There are moose warnings along the highways. Moose silhouettes on sweatshirts. Paintings of moose on garages and barns. Little plush mooses in gift shops. Sorry … shoppes. The beloved friends with whom my wife, Shelly, and I were staying even took us on an afternoon ramble along dirt roads in search of bona fide moose. We saw none, but in a village diner I enjoyed a cup of potato soup. I was thinking of that earlier cup when my latest cup arrived. Another potato soup. Steaming, creamy, exquisite. With a mysterious, faint crunch. I closed my eyes in pleasure and wondered, *Is that a* dinosaur *crunch?* Well, no. *Just the crackers,* I added.

I paid my tab—$1.95—and rose to leave. My gaze fell on one final hand-lettered sign. It was on the coat rack. The sign said, "Coat Rack." I wasn't surprised. Remember: I was in a professional building.

'Mong the Hills of Cattaraugus . . .

... stands the school we love so well.
We have spent such happy hours,
Ever more our praises tell ...

I don't live in Little Valley anymore. It sits "'mong the hills" of Cattaraugus County. In western New York State. Those hills are round and lovely. Those hills are a delight. Little Valley is literal: the village is small and situated between mountains (well, hills) that bubbled up some Mesozoic millennia ago. And those hills welcome forests (which we Little Valley-ites call *woods*). Enough trees were cleared to make meadows to grow corn and wheat to feed the pretty-eyed cows to give their milk to the Dairymen's League to sell to homes and schools to serve to children ... milk from a nearby farm with its numbing, whewing icy-cold.

That "school we loved so well"—from kindergarten through twelfth grade—was a two-story brick structure fronting Main Street and following the bend on Thompson Avenue. An unremarkable building. Except to us, its students. To us it was a center, a focus, an inconvenience, a delight, a gathering of pals and romance, a looming presence that we could never ignore. Even in summer as we hair-flyingly pedaled our bicycles past it. And remembering it now (which I do often), that school building is one of my favorite places.

I remember every teacher who taught me. Taught us. In kindergarten it

5

was Beatrice Harder. Bea. Bea Harder. Which sounds more like a motto than a name. First teacher to severely scold me. Not the last. I pressed bottle caps into the radiator fan—which made a loud, mesmerizing (or, to Mrs. Harder, annoying) rattle—in our oddly shaped classroom. And because I was one of the few who had not learned yet to tie my shoes, there was a construction paper cutout of a shoe with dangling laces up on the bulletin board announcing my ignominy. My brother, Harlow, wound up teaching me how to accomplish the task one day after school. He insisted that I learn to tie my shoes or he wouldn't let me climb *up* and roll *down* the dirt bank across the creek behind our house. I loved dirt. Still do. Oh, and in Little Valley we say *crick*.

First grade was conducted by Elsie Gorsline, one of the kindest people in history. And she always had a picnic at her house on Fair Oak Street at the end of the school year. In the other first grade—Mrs. Holtz's—a print of Grant Wood's *The Midnight Ride of Paul Revere* hung on the wall. I fell in love with that painting when we'd visit the "other" first grade for a slideshow about squirrels or to practice diving under our desks for when Russia bombed us.

It was in Arlene Eighme's second grade that my buddy Bobby Miller (to whom this book is dedicated) started smoking. He could put away a pack of Marlboros while Mrs. Eighme read a chapter of *Winnie the Pooh*.

Third grade was something of a disappointment. Mrs. Remington (Helen Remington, who later married Charlie Wilcox and became Mrs. Wilcox. I just want to be certain you have all the information to save you from googling my claims). I was severely challenged in third-grade arithmetic. That's a word you hear no more. *Arithmetic.* And I am glad. *Arithmetic* was, for me, a synonym for *drudgery*, for *enemy*. I was often sent out into the hall to "work" on my deficiency with numbers. I spent more time in the hall than Harold Gloff, our friendly school custodian.

That summer I underwent an appendectomy from which I received a cool scar and permission in Eleanor Hogan's fourth grade to stand and walk around my desk ... any time I desired. It was Miss Hogan's idea. And I embraced it.

Fifth grade—under the tutelage of Ruth Currie—was another downer sort of year. We were combined with the sixth grade and always had a spelling test on Friday. Mrs. Currie announced one Friday that if everyone achieved a 100, she'd treat us all to ice cream. On that ominous day there was only one word misspelled by one student: me. The word was "exercise." I've always had trouble with that word. And concept.

Ruth Miller's sixth grade had mixed moments. During a lesson one sunny afternoon, I spat a glob of spit on a map of Spain in our geography book. It was a cool, clear, perfectly circular glob of spit (which was a delighting surprise and made me feel proud). Well. I had not noticed Mr. Memmott—our principal for all the years from kindergarten through senior graduation—standing in the doorway. Seeing me spit on a venerable textbook. He slowly approached my desk and, looming (Mr. Memmott was expert at looming), instructed me to take my handkerchief and wipe up the spit. I obeyed. And pulled from my pocket one of my mother's frilly, flowery handkerchiefs in which she had tied my lunch money. Bobby Miller saw the pink and purple lace and the edges of the handkerchief's silky substance ... and fell out of his seat laughing. And broke several Marlboros in his pocket when he landed.

But it was also in Mrs. Miller's sixth grade that I met *Huckleberry Finn* and *David Copperfield*. She introduced us to them with lunch-hour readings over the course of the school year.

On to junior high and Hazel Smith's seventh grade. She was a fervent Republican, and the day after the 1960 presidential election—November 9, 1960—she chewed out our entire class because John Kennedy had won. I guess we deserved it. I would have voted for JFK, but I couldn't. I was in the seventh grade.

Eighth grade was led by Evelyn Sharpe. As nice a woman who ever gave anyone detention. Well, one afternoon Pat—Mr. Memmott's secretary—stopped me as I walked by the office and asked me to take a stack of forms to Mrs. Sharpe to be distributed to her students. When I arrived at her classroom, it was empty. So I placed a note on her desk with the stack of forms. The note said, "Mrs. Sharpe: please pass out." I reworked my wording later that day on detention.

Ninth grade was high school in Little Valley, and that's when Miss Buck came into my life. Miss Buck. Marylu Buck. I developed a serious crush on Miss Buck. Along with all of the other guys at Little Valley Central. Miss Buck. Sigh.

John Feneran taught English in my sophomore year, and I recall that he was sad on the January day in 1963 when Robert Frost died. I didn't understand at the time. I understand now.

I studied *biology* in Addie Belle Willard's *chemistry* lab (we were cramped in that old building). To say I "studied" biology is an affront to the verb *studied*. I occupied a seat and tried my best to entertain away the gravitas of science. In the middle of one of my particularly laugh-inducing monologues, Mrs. Willard interrupted her lecture (on the paramecium) ... and smacked me over the head with a rubber-tipped wooden pointer (with which she had been pointing out the paramecium's cilia) and expressed a furious hope that I would get over fool's hill. Hell, I'm still climbing it.

It was in Paul Felton's eleventh-grade English class that I fell in love with something even more beautiful than Miss Buck: poetry. I've been reading it and writing it ever since. It was in that class that I first understood the sadness at Robert Frost's death. Bless you, Mr. Felton.

In twelfth grade we were graced by one of the nicest human beings to ever stroll the planet: Rodney Lounsbury. Our homeroom teacher. And he taught us typing. Great thing for a writer and a journalist. Great thing for any of us. It connected our imaginings—through our fingers—to words. Ah, good old home keys: A S D F J K L ;

I've mentioned Mr. Memmott. Arthur Memmott. He seemed to be the tallest man in the world. Stationed—as we rushed through the two minutes between classes—at the door to his office. Mr. Memmott. Arms folded. Countenance fixed and scholarly and stern. You didn't dare break step as you flowed past him. One morning, as I was in that hectic flow flowing from Algebra to American History, Emmie Danks was walking behind me. And threw up. On my back. I didn't even slow down. Just kept moving on to American History. Mr. Memmott frowned on us vomiting. Our kind and smiling custodian Harold Gloff (whom we met when I was back in the third grade struggling with arithmetic and banished to the hall, remember?) joined the line and sprinkled some of that hairy brown vomit-soaker-upper on my shirt, while his custodial colleague Erlen Waite broomed me off. All on the way to history.

Oh, the school memories of cherished Little Valley and the teachers who lifted our lives: Edward Jedzerek—"Jed"—taught shop. I still have the lamp I fashioned under his tutelage on a lathe from a soft pine cylinder. Shelly insists I keep it in the closet. But I love that lamp and sometimes take it out and plug it in and read an "Archie" comic book. Just because. Thank you, Jed.

There was Mr. Connelly, the guidance counselor (whose Volkswagen we wedged between trees at the bowling alley one ill-advised autumn evening). And Coach Thornton Newhouse, who insisted we climb those damned ropes in gym. Well, insisted we *try* to climb them. To this day I harbor a strong hatred of ropes. And there was Coach Lou Bartolotti, who kicked me off the football team for breaking curfew. It was the night before a big game, and the entire shame-on-me episode is related in other pages in this volume.

All the years I was in school in Little Valley, the music teacher was Mrs. Bartow—*Onolee* Bartow (worth knowing for her name alone). She played organ at all the June commencements. And when I was in second grade she noted how dreadful I was at singing. Years later I danced and acted—*and sang*—in *The Fantasticks* and *Joseph and the Amazing Technicolor Dreamcoat* in New York and Connecticut. I always wished Mrs. Bartow had been in the audience.

Another science teacher, with whom I had a better rapport than with Mrs. Willard, was Donald Krug. He actually made science interesting. And studyable. And he smiled. And coached the junior varsity basketball team (of which I was not a member, since I had stopped growing when I was struggling with third-grade arithmetic). He actually seemed interested in our lives and thoughts. And he never once admonished me to get over fool's hill.

And there was Mr. Keenen—Tom Keenen—one of the smartest, kindest, funniest, most encouraging people to ever sweeten our lives. He taught American History. And had impeccable penmanship. His musings on the blackboard were works of art. I still remember every Friday—because of the weekly current-affairs exam. He named Friday W.O.B. Day: "Weed Out the Bluffers." We were in Mr. Keenen's afternoon class on Friday, November 22, 1963. News of the murder of President Kennedy in Dallas reached us on the loudspeaker in the classroom. I'll never forget seeing Mr. Keenen—an Irish Catholic Democrat—drop his head to his desk and cry. Every year when November 22 arrives in the cold autumn I think, of course, of President Kennedy. And Mr. Keenen.

School was the bubble and fizz of our lives. The dances and romances. The "game nights" on winter Wednesdays when we would roller-skate for an hour and then—when the gymnasium lights dimmed—dance for another hour to 45 rpm records. The Twist. The Monkey. Mashed Potato. Loco-Motion. No wonder I have had both hips replaced and have undergone two knee surgeries and discectomy in my aching back. Bless you, Chubby Checker.

But Little Valley was more than school. Little Valley was a village of sunshine and shadows. Shadows beneath trees in the daylight. Shadows over and under every place at night. And I loved the shadows of Little Valley. We fell in love and kissed in the summer shadows. We rode the snow on sleds under clouds in winter. We fell in love and walked through the ice-sparkled air holding hands and crunching through the cold to a kiss on a porch.

You could not trip on a shadow. A shadow can't alter your step. It plays with light ... light that must *be* there for the shadow to *be* there. Was a shadow a worry? A fear? A hiding place for menace and threat? Yes. And a shadow is for hiding, cozying, and comforting tucking-away.

I said at the start of this meditation, "I don't live in Little Valley anymore." That's not true. I live in Little Valley in my mind and heart still. And visit it every day.

Music, Music, Music

Music. I love it. Easy statement. Unchallenged. Unchallengeable. Who doesn't love music? Seriously. Who doesn't? No one doesn't. Well, before I tangle negatives intended as positives and sprain my syntax, let's spend a minute musing on music.

Do you recall your first melody? I don't recall mine. Songs are like breaths and the scent of sausage in a warm morning kitchen. Songs simply sit in the air waiting to be noticed and juggled upon the ear. It's easier on the imagination to learn what goes into making a song than what goes into making sausage. *Ick* isn't a term that emerges from a discussion of music.

I remember when my parents bought the family's first television. But there was always a radio. On a sill by the stove. And a large console on the floor of the living room. (Which we never called "the living room"; it was always "the front room." I suppose we intended to live in all the rooms of the house so there was no need to designate just one for living.) We also had a record player. Remember one of those? And its terms: *spindle, rpm,* and *45.* We had two records in my parents' house. The Chordettes' version of "Mr. Sandman" (a 78 rpm record) and an album (33 and 1/3 rpm) of hymns by Tennessee Ernie Ford. The whole family rather liked the harmonies by the Chordettes. But Ol' Ern was the artistic passion of my dad. That and bowling.

My older brothers, Larry and Harlow, started bringing home rock-and-roll in the late '50s. Fats Domino. Some Elvis. A dash of Dion and the Belmonts. Connie Francis. Neil Sedaka; always sounded like decaffeinated coffee to me. "A cup o' Sedaka to go, please." I pretty much wrested control of the record player from Tennessee Ernie and the others when I heard and wound up buying Joey Dee and the Starliters and Bobby Rydell and Chubby Checker and (here a reverent pause, please ...) the Beatles. Saw them on Ed Sullivan that February night in 1964 and I was transported. Transfixed. Transformed. Wow. *Wow* doesn't come close to my actual reaction to the Beatles. It remains ineffable. Always will. My father's reaction, however, was effable. Completely and earthily effable. But not printable. I'll bet even Tennessee Ernie Ford blushed on the album jacket beside the record player when my father raged at the sight of John, Paul, George, and Ringo on the "rilly big shew." But I loved them. And have ever since. From *Meet the Beatles!* right on through *Revolver* and the "White Album" to *Sgt. Pepper, Abbey Road*, and *Let It Be*. The Beatles. Wow.

My taste is eclectic. My record collection included the Kingston Trio, the Chad Mitchell Trio, the Dave Clark Five (the numbers in the names were the closest I ever came to understanding math), the Limelighters, Joe and Eddie. And I've dug Sinatra and George Shearing and Pete Fountain and the Village Stompers (ever hear their "Limehouse Blues"? Stunning). Rosemary Clooney. Roy Orbison. And on to the classical: Mahler, *Dvořák* (who gets so many sounds out of so few letters in a name? ... no wonder he was a composer), Delius, Tchaikovsky, Ralph Vaughan Williams (and Ralph is pronounced "Rafe." Ah, the Brits).

Music. It's always in my mind. Always in the air.

Unreal Estate

The house-for-sale tour. Now, there's an experience. It begins with a ride in the real estate agent's car. I like traveling in my own car. My car is neither cool nor neat. Shelly calls it downright filthy. There's a scatter of M&M's. The errant Cheeto. Cracker shrapnel. And books. And CDs. Old cassette tapes. I am afraid to dig into the rubble. Afraid I might find some frightening thing. A neglected bill. A petrified burger. An annoyed hamster. The real estate agent's car is always newer and bigger than mine. And smells of lavender-and-mint. A little pine-tree-shaped gahingus dangles from the rearview mirror, flitting its fragrance into the leather interior and over the faux-wood instrument panel. My car doesn't smell of lavender-and-mint. My car is redolent of snacks. And desserts. And hors d'oeuvres. And the lost sock. The odor of mint would be confronted at the door by the resident odors; it would be bullied—with a sniff and a scowl—to "Hit the road, mint. You ain't welcome here." I never let anyone ride in my car who is more than ten years away from their last tetanus shot. In the real estate agent's car I feel like I ought to be wearing a cashmere cardigan or a tweed jacket with suede elbow patches. And shoes with tassels. I feel like I ought to be addressing people as "Biff" and "chum." And asking about their time at the Cape. And remarking on what a blessing lavender-and-mint is.

We pull up to the target house and slow to a crawl at the "For Sale" sign. I know the real estate agent is admiring the name and phone number hooked at the bottom of the sign. Yep. Cool, minty lettering. At this point we're told, "This is the driveway. Paved." Now, I am no MIT-educated transportation engineer, but I can spot a blacktopped driveway pretty quickly. And hedges.

You don't need to point out those bushes along that driveway. I know hedges and bushes. I've mowed a lawn or three in my day.

"This is the flagstone sidewalk," we're told as we walk along the flagstone sidewalk. I think somebody sends out memos to real estate agents that say I am stupid. The flagstone sidewalk leads to the lockbox on the front door. "This is the lockbox," reveals the agent. I want to answer, "And this is—let me guess—the front door?" But I don't. I am finishing a sneeze from the last sniff of lavender-and-mint.

We step inside to "Here's our foyer." We haven't even signed any papers, but already the foyer is ours. Some places it's a FOY-er, and some places it's a foy-YAY. The agent points to the light fixture above and I think, "Chandelier." The agent says, "Chandelier." And I think, "Yes! Got it!" Shelly frowns at me. And I wonder if I thought that thought out loud.

We step into the first room off to the left. It features a stove, a refrigerator, a table surrounded by chairs, and pots and pans hanging from a rack above the stove. I am thinking "Kitchen" as the agent intones, "This is the kitchen." Real estate agents must think the people to whom they are showing a house have never been inside a house. They must think we come from a rock or a lean-to in the forest. The agent identifies that place with the sink and toilet as "your bathroom." And the wiggly-glassed booth with the shower nozzle and drain is "your shower."

We move woefully slowly down the hall and step into a wide, long place sporting a bed and nightstands and a closet with enough space for Rhode Island. I'm mentally sorting through my house terms when the agent breaks the suspense by saying, "And this is your bedroom." That's it! Bedroom! Oh, I almost had it. Yes, bedroom. Now I remember.

And on we go to other exotic places: down the stairs to the "finished basement." Never, ever refer to the basement as "the cellar." The only "seller" is the family who wants you to buy the house you're touring. There is the "family room" and "bonus room" and "guest room." I'd like there to be a place large enough for storing cleaning tools, for meditating, for combing your hair, for practicing drums, for keeping an Egyptian sarcophagus, for discussing eschatology, and for weaving. I'd call it the "broom, groom, boom-boom, tomb, doom, loom, and ruminating room." And it'd smell of lavender-and-mint.

I think we'll just stay where we are.

Butterflies and Things . . .

As I walked down the driveway from fetching the paper this autumn morn, the sky was iron gray and seeping a chill into the air and me. The grand maple in our front yard has gone from green to gold to bare-branched ... in what seems like the blink of a barn swallow's eye. The leaves lay strewn and still on the leaning-into-sleep grass. I like the fall. I like it so much I usually refer to it as "autumn." Out of respect and awe. Awe-tumn. But there is no mistaking the season's intention. It evicts heat. It frowns on wading at the beach or creek. Autumn is what Archibald MacLeish calls "the human season" ... it reminds us of our mortality.

So, I was delighted to settle in at my trusty computer and visit InteriorDesign.net. Its prosaic name belies its poetic effect. And the name serves itself well by taking me *in* to places. There *is* the occasional nod to *exteriors*, as well. Designed or nature-authored. And even when we are *in*side ... we're often spurred to ponder *out*side things. Like butterflies.

InteriorDesign.net ushered me to the "Butterfly Pavilion" which sits in Washington, D.C. The photos are enchanting. The pavilion is shaped like a giant cocoon rising twelve feet high and weaving wispy and white and silk-like to suggest that a caterpillar might have headed the design team using material air-kissed from the sweetly named "3form." In one photo a giggling huddle of children pauses in a field trip at some inviting scene seen inside the pavilion. As it should be. As it should be when it comes to children and butterflies. They're only too briefly together. For these enterprises we have come to resort to such adjectives as *interactive* and *educational*. That's what happens to us adults when we reach the age of leaving butterflies behind. We aim for the interactive and the educational. All a child needs is a butterfly. And all a butterfly needs is to be noticed or ignored or imagined or respected. It begins its career as a larva, then moves on to caterpillar status to spend some study time before graduating with dusty wings and flitting flights from flower to flower around the neighborhood, around the continent.

InteriorDesign.net speaks of the challenge designers faced "to emulate the appearance of a caterpillar's silk cocoon" for the pavilion's "butterfly display." What was required was "material with ethereal qualities" like "the delicate silk" that a caterpillar spins. Some great words fueled this endeavor: "silk," "ethereal," "delicate," and one of the best of words: "butterfly." The design evolved into an environment. An environment to be visited by mesmerized children (of any age) and to be inhabited by fragile, beautiful butterflies. And plants and rocks ... gently lighted. The enterprise becomes technical here and I confess to a complete lack of knowledge about Varia EcoResin and how it is "Greenguard Indoor Air Quality Certified." Even the selected color—"Evo White"—is beyond my ken. I understand "white" because I am a lover of snow. But "Evo" is a mystery. A happy, engaging mystery, but a mystery. Robert Frost knew of butterflies and things. In his "The Tuft of Flowers" he watches a butterfly's "noiseless" and "tremulous wing[s]." Poet and butterfly light upon "a message from the dawn" that invites hearing the songs of birds and the whisper of a scythe harvesting hay. And how we all ought to work together. And can. To work together, we have to get along with each other.

So a butterfly pavilion isn't just lovely in design and structure. It is a lovely idea. And now there's a Butterfly Pavilion in America's capitol. There ought to be one in every nation's capitol. For children to visit. Thanks, InteriorDesign.net, for suggesting it.

Well, Picture That

T. S. Eliot is a whiner. April isn't cruel. It's magical. As I have mentioned elsewhere, April is Poetry Month. Because tradition has it, history's finest poet, William Shakespeare, was born in 1564 on April 23 and died in 1616, also on April 23. A solemn symmetry.

Back in '06—2006—a portrait was discovered in England that suggested it was a during-his-life depiction of Shakespeare. The so-called Cobbe portrait has been determined to have been painted in the early seventeenth century, while the Bard was still striding the globe (and the Globe, his theater in London), a successful playwright and actor. And nattily dressed as important people were wont to be in Olde Englande in those olde days.

The man in the oil-on-wood picture is slimmer than the Shakespeare we've known from the engraving by Martin Droeshout featured on the First Folio of plays that Shakespeare's fellow King's Men actors John Heminges and Henry Condell arranged to publish after the Bard died. And considerably more svelte than the marble bust guarding his grave in the church at Stratford-upon-Avon. This new-to-the-light likeness features a long face with a tapering chin and a wisp of goatee. He stares confidently at you, at me, as we regard his countenance. *Is* it confidence, or a sober mien from mild discomfort at the ruff ringing his neck? That thing must have required a good dose of starch to maintain its crisp shape and attitude. And *that* had to involve some serious itching.

The buttons on the waistcoat? There are eleven visible (in the Droeshout engraving there are twelve and a half), but I am betting they continue beyond the bottom of the portrait right down to the—I also bet—ballooned thigh-length trousers from which hose-encased legs lead to a pair of snazzy shoes. With buckles. All the rage with Laurence Olivierand Errol Flynn back in the '40s—the *1940s*. I am certainly no expert (as I write, I wear blue jeans and a green flannel shirt stained with soup or spinach dip), but the material looks to be a blue-black velvet embroidered with gold thread piping. (I had to pause to laugh at this attempt to fake my way through this description).

And while having a generous dome of a forehead, the fellow in the Cobbe portrait sports a nice thatch of dark brown hair. He isn't bald and puffy as Droeshout would have him. I am going to believe that the picture is, indeed, William Shakespeare. I'll not give credence to the doubters, the conspiracy theorists who cry, "That's not him!"—elitists who also wail that Shakespeare could not possibly have written the poems and plays that bear his byline. They question how a lowly-born son of a common glover in a town named Stratford (the word *Podunk* had not yet been coined) could ever have created Falstaff and Prince Hal and Prospero and Ophelia and Oberon and Titania and Puck. How could such a hick give literary life to Juliet and her cherished Romeo? A lunkhead from the woodsy banks of the River Avon penning the revels and rivalries of wealthy Verona, the court*room* in Venice or the court*yards* of kings in England and Denmark and Scotland? However could a blue-ruff groundling write of kings and things? Imagination, you snob. *Imagination.* A mightier attribute than inheritance or nobility or weekends at a castle peopled with people named "Lady" and "Sir." Mightier by far than all those considerations combined.

Sorry about the rant. But I just love Shakespeare. We've known for centuries how he *thought*. I am thrilled now to know how he *looked*. I'm convinced the Cobbe portrait is our Shakespeare. And a pal told me not long ago that *he saw that very picture* on the piano in Mom and Pop Shakespeare's living room.

Noisy Is the Night

"He must be very rich," said John simply.
I'm glad. I like very rich people.
"The richer a fella is, the better I like him."

—

"The simple piety prevalent in Hades has the
earnest worship of and respect for riches as the first
article of its creed ... "

—F. Scott Fitzgerald
The Diamond as Big as the Ritz

It's another night as so many this winter past, filled with fog. A fog that doesn't rise, doesn't swirl. A fog that just hugs the ground close, hangs in the air, and muffles all noise. It's a night to get out of. I step into Miranda's ...

My eyes have no trouble adjusting to the nearly dark restaurant. The place is all ferns and white latticework. Intimate booths and multi-levels for dining. Long-stemmed wine glasses catch the little light and compress and elongate it.

I don't have a reservation at the restaurant. I have an appointment.

"I'm here to see Mitch," I tell the slender—and taller than I—hostess. She's a beautiful person. The first of many I'll see this night.

"And your name, sir?" Her eyebrows arch. Even in this shadowy atmosphere, I can see her eyeshadow seductively wisped across heavy, lovely lids.

Waiting to meet the owner, I settle on a straight-back padded bench and allow my eyes to roam the room. Some diners peer languidly at me over their meals. I don't arouse any interest and they return to their intimate little worlds. The window tables are enchanting. Candles and their tiny yellow flames; from outside, a streetlamp offers a softened illumination through the fog, through the tall windows to the diners and their tidy tables. The glass panes give the fog and the night a bottled aspect, and I'm allowing the gloomy weather another chance to be liked when I sniff an expensive cologne and feel someone beside me. It's the man I've come to see.

"I'm Mitch." His right hand reaches out. In his other hand is a squat tumbler of some clear liquid and rattling ice.

Mitch is slender, athletic-looking. Peter Fonda with a mustache. He has the angularity of someone with a lot of free time. His eyes are only three-quarters open and his head dips slightly forward, chin first. He looks like I have interrupted his sleep, but I haven't. He has been awake since morning. And he will stay awake long into the morning to come.

Men who *have* dreams *don't* dream. There isn't time.

We decide to chat in Mitch's second-floor office. On our way to the stairs, he greets some regular patrons and calls the waiter aside for a hasty, hushed conversation. I assume he's giving his employee some Simon and Garfunkel "keep the customer satisfied" advice. A perfunctory tour reveals the delights on that second floor—a private dining room, festooned ceiling and wall with infinity mirrors and furnished with mirror-topped tables plus an honest-to-goodness plastic palm tree that looks stolen from an old Adolphe Menjou motion picture. Then there's a backgammon lounge, tables adorned with inlaid boards that have attracted a few players. Mitch ushers me through a reception area and into his office. A rough, masculine alcove with high ceilings and woven wood blinds over the windows. Two walls are covered by pictures—pictures of my host. My host with a variety of people. A variety of things. Cars, boats, jets. Seated at fancy nightclub tables. And always with beautiful people.

Mitch sits at his desk. I sit in a big wicker sort-of-egg that surrounds my sides and back and curves over my head. My gaze falls upon a pair of cockatiels—exotic birds with beautiful plumage—while their eyes observe me with a nervous flutter. The Caribbean effect is complete.

I'm here to see a discotheque. Gauche fellow that I am, I call it a "disco." Mitch detests the term. I'm at a loss for a better one. Anyway, the whatever-you-call-it is on the floor above us, and before I see it, my host wants to explain it. You don't enter a discotheque lightly. At least Mitch doesn't.

There's a "Once upon a time" tinge to the story he relates, the story of the *Third Floor* at *Miranda's. It begins in 1965 in Acapulco ...*

... the discotheque was finding its form in the cosmos. The amoeba was getting its legs and learning not to walk, but to dance.

According to Mitch, *the* place for dancing in 1965 in Acapulco was Renaldo's Le Club, a posh nightspot that first tantalized him not because of its inside beauty, but because he couldn't *get inside.* He tried once. Sorry. He tried again. Nope. But he kept trying until he ... got ... in. And when he reached the inside, Mitch began to vibrate like a tuning fork. To the fever of disco.

He found a friend—"My Mexican brother," Mitch calls him: Ramon. A fellow who rose in the Acapulco disco strata because of his passion for that lifestyle and the driving, dancing frenzy that fueled it. Like the lovers of the bullfight in Hemingway's *The Sun Also Rises,* "These men were aficionados ... it amused them very much." On the second-floor office wall are pictures of Mitch and Ramon, the Prince of Acapulco, laughing at nightlife tables, basking in soft club light.

Mitch's conversation—er, monologue—is laced with the names of jet-set stomping grounds: The Cow, in Buenos Aires; Anabel's in London; the Candy Store and Bumbles in Los Angeles; Regine's in Monte Carlo; Studio 54 in New York. Discotheques that sprang up in the shower of money spent on throbbing music. Loud, luring, seducing.

As I sense my anticipated visit to the *Third Floor* nearing, Mitch shows a side that surprises me after all the talk that's gone before—humility.

"Mitch couldn't have done it alone," he admits, slipping into the third

22

person.

He tells me of the efforts of Lorraine, his mother, a designer, to whom he is deeply devoted. She has done international work for, among others, Far East Lines (she designed three passenger ships), Harrod's Department Store in Buenos Aires, a number of airlines. Mitch speaks about a lighting consultant, Donald, who carried a retail wallpaper store to impressive heights. Mitch sings the praises of Augusto, a pioneer in quadraphonic sound. If you're building a stadium to seat a hundred thousand people or a disco for dancing, Augusto—and he's expensive, they say—is the man to call for sound. He helped Mitch with planning the intricate speaker network. It took seven months at a laboratory in Livermore, California, to wire the computer (that orchestrates the show I'm about to see), and Kevin, the wizard who accomplished it. The disc jockey, Marc, is local talent. Formerly a clerk at an appliance store, Kevin supplied the expertise for installing the elaborate sound system after doing field research in Acapulco—all expenses paid by Mitch. Converting the *Third Floor* from individual hotel rooms to a dance palace fell on the shoulders of a local construction company. And Darrell—renowned as "the Mirror-Man"—arranged the looking glasses that cover the walls.

These are, as Mitch calls them, "the magic people." The ones who took neon and spotlights and color and with a kind of future-shock alchemy ... made electric gold; the ones who wove the sound system into the room and into the very bodies of the dancers. These artistic technicians are the ones who have computerized sound and computerized sight to make the *Third Floor* the loud and lighted mirror palace of dance and narcissism it is.

And so, finally, I am about the spend an evening in the rarefied atmosphere of the discotheque above Stevens Street. Mitch advises me to come back later: ten or ten-thirty. "That's when the wildness starts." When I tell Shelly that I'm going to the disco at ten-thirty on a Friday night, she asks me if I want to nap for a couple of hours before I go.

So ... when I trudge up two flights of stairs that Friday night, I am greeted by a tuxedoed waiter. There's a strict dress code on the *Third Floor*. A letter sent to desired customers before opening states, "In order to maintain proper attire compatible with our surroundings, we expressly prohibit the following modes of dress: jeans, khakis, corduroys or other casual trousers, athletic shoes of any type, shorts, men's hats, ladies' informal blouses and like clothing. Determination of the suitability of any questionable form of dress shall be entirely at the discretion of the management."

My solid brown pants and plaid jacket get me past the checkpoint, *Tuxedo Junction*, and up the second flight of stairs (lighted on each step by little recessed theater bulbs) and into the *Third Floor*. A place with more than sixteen miles of wiring, more than six thousand lights, fifty speakers, and an "independent" thirty-two-channel computerized amplifier system. The Corian dance floor (dotted around its edges with colored lights) is filled with bouncing humanity like the fiesta celebrants in *The Sun Also Rises*: "The dancers were in a crowd, so you did not see the intricate play of the feet. All you saw was the heads and shoulders going up and down." My brown plaid follows the tuxedo to the table I'll occupy 'til closing time.

The mirror panels—more than four thousand—make the twenty-four hundred square feet of fun-seeking seem larger and more thickly populated. After a few minutes at my table, I'm wishing they'd cut a few corners and bought fewer than *fifty* speakers. The music is slick, clear—all the highs and the proper bass. It's just so damned ... loud. Ah, but maybe I'm being unfair—I've not had my nap.

I look at the dancers. I want to see fun. Thousands and thousands of dollars have been lavished *on* this playground to entice revelers to spend thousands and thousands *in* it. Mitch isn't worried about the investment because, he says, "It makes a beautiful party."

I feel more than a little like Nick Carraway to his Great Gatsby. I'm an outsider in this music mansion where, as Fitzgerald puts it, "... the lights grow brighter as the earth lurches away from the sun ..."

I'm surprised at the gray hair, white hair, thinning hair in the gyrating crowd. Mitch estimates the average age of his partying customers to be thirty-five or forty. These are the people he enjoys seeing enjoy themselves. "The bluebloods," Mitch calls them. I watch the bluebloods with plain old O positive coursing through *my* veins.

The dancers, early in the evening, are self-conscious. There are the beginnings of smiles on their faces. Tentative, testing smiles. Like a swimmer's toe touching the pool before plunging. They dance ... or move in what is now taken for dancing. And I think of how my father would react to all this noise and undulation. He who claimed that my little six-transistor AM pocket radio hastened him to near deafness.

The music is unrelenting. The bass beat jiggles the condensation on the chilled champagne buckets at neighboring tables. Live orchestras, big bands, and rock groups all take intermissions. Disco does not. A record needs no rest. But the dancers ... don't they need a break?

The lights are fun. They make me wonder if Mutual of Omaha has retina insurance, but they *are* fun. Blue, white, red, big, small, neon, strobe. They're lightning and the music is thunder. There's *really* a whole lot o' shakin' goin' on—shakin' and blinkin' and yellin'. Conversation is impossible. But then, who goes to Studio 54 to chat?

The music shifts to a slower tempo. This happens only three or four times a night. That's when the blue lights do their solos and weave the eve with a nice romantic ocean-wave ebb and flow ... above the *now embracing* dancers.

But ... slow music diminishes the number of dancers. And if there isn't dancing, there isn't disco. There is *listening*. You can listen at home. So the music pats the computer on the gigabyter and that yanks all the lights back to the party, back to life, pop, slam, wham, pow. It's back to business. Back to frenzy.

The festive folk, I notice, steal frequent glances in the mirrors. They appear to like what they see. Because they continue looking. And the lights reflect in everything—the mirrors, the glasses, the champagne bottles, the eyes of the dancers, the eyes of the watchers, the keys of the cash register.

As the night dins on, cigarette smoke climbs the shafts of light, and I find myself talking about Margaret Trudeau and Mexico and banking. Topics about which I know nothing. From those around me I hear such words as "mellow" and "far out" and "super" and "magic" and "bitchin'" and "heavy." I'm invited to dance, but I keep firmly seated. I just want to be one of the people, not one of the dancers. Besides, I haven't had my nap.

There's atmosphere in the *Third Floor*. Elegant, fashionable, glittering, dazzling, but the thread of it all is heavy and weighted with dollar signs. It's a hell of a party. But not everyone is invited.

Finally (and for a while it didn't seem inevitable), 1:45 of a new morning arrives and the last note of Donna Summer's "Last Dance" echoes off the mirrors. The thousand-dollar lights blink out and are replaced by the anticlimactic illumination of hundred-watt Sylvania soft-whites. The beautiful people are done dancing, and faint circles are seen beneath their eyes. Coffee is brought around on trays by servers still wearing their *Godfather* tuxedos.

A patron approaches Mitch and playfully criticizes the dress code. "I don't mind telling you I felt a little silly tonight after I closed my place at eleven o'clock, hung my jeans on a hanger, and put on some slacks just so you'd let me in here." Mitch smiles, half amused, like Gatsby, he "had waited five years and bought a mansion where he dispensed starlight to casual moths." *All* moths like light, but only a few ever get close enough to feel its warmth. It must be strange to hear these privileged moths close to the light complaining about having to dress the part.

The mad dancing in the electric night had its embryonic stirrings in the Jazz Age of Fitzgerald, who wasn't just writing about the flapper and her beau, but some primal human craving for distraction: "then the glow faded, each light deserting her with lingering regret, like children leaving a pleasant street at dusk." All of us were leaving now. I clumped down the stairs into the aging, still foggy night and slipped into my car. Three floors above me lights were blinking out and staying out, and dust was settling through its monied air.

II

Thieving. Safety. Cliosophy

Crime at the DMV

Sigh. As we were heading into town for ice cream, a blue light pulled me over: 42 in a 30-mph zone. A fumble in the glove compartment for my automobubble's registration revealed that the registration had expired ... three years ago. Gulp. It's never good to gulp in front of a cop who has just pulled you over. It can invite a Breathalyzer. But we were on our way to the ice cream parlor, not the tavern, so I was far below the legal limit for alcohol. But over the top in anticipation of sea-salt-caramel-swirl. He was a local officer—and friendly—so he suggested that I call the DMV in the morning to "clear this up."

So. Call I did. And I was told to report immediately to the office in Danbury. So. Report I did. I waited behind five people at the first station just inside the door. Waited for a severe white-haired woman to present a little printed ticket that gave me access to the next station, "Information." Seven people ahead of me there. When I finally reached her, the information lady was welcoming and smiley. But she frowned at my expired registration and exhaled, "Ooo." It wasn't a sea-salt-caramel-swirl "Ooo." It was a "You're a knucklehead and in a lot of trouble Ooo." And with a nod of her now frowning head, I was directed to the hundred uncomfortable chairs area to wait for my number—C768—to be called over the scratchy DMV loudspeaker.

When I was a little boy I vowed to never be bored. So Wiffle ball, Welsh Corgis, toss-and-catch, McDonald's, skipping-stones-over-a-lake, Welsh Corgis, spitting, hoping to kiss girls, Fowler's Taffy at the Cattaraugus County Fair, and Welsh Corgis helped me to keep that vow. Then, when two hip replacements ended my Wiffle ball and toss-and-catch career; and when I moved away from lakes; when it was pointed out that spitting is pretty disgusting and would kill any hope I had for kissing girls; when I lost three fillings to Fowler's Taffy at the Cattaraugus County Fair; when all that was left was a Welsh Corgi, I grew to rely on books to keep boredom at bay. Nothing better than sitting with a good book and reaching down to scruffle the fur of a sleeping-by-your-chair Welsh Corgi to keep boredom at bay.

So ...

... I had Philip Levine's memoirs to help me endure the wait for the next available clerk or attendant or DMV person. I read. I waited. I checked the time. Five minutes. I read. I waited. Twelve minutes. I waited and I read and thirty-two minutes groaned on the DMV clock. I read Philip Levine's memories of jazz and musicians in Detroit. An hour of my life sighed out of my life and I waited. The DMV loudspeaker scratched scratchier and scratchier. Time oozed like lazy lava.

Then, "C768, please go to window 6." And so I went. To Window 6. A fellow named Hugh. I proffered my expired registration, title, and driver's license. Hugh pushed his lower lip up over his upper lip and lifted his eyebrows north as he examined my proffering. He handed me a complicated form to complete. I had no pen. There was a nice ballpoint on Hugh's counter, so I picked it up and started writing in the form's little boxes.

"Your registration is expired."

"Yes. It's why I am here. To un-expire it, Hugh." I thought a little play on words and friendly use of his name might lower Hugh's eyebrows and relax his lower lip. I returned to completing the form with Hugh's ballpoint pen as he riffled through the paperwork and clacked on his computer and began to slowly, to s-l-o-w-l-y shake his head. Pretty much everything at the DMV gets hyphens in the s-l-o-w-l-i-e-s. Hugh squinted. Hugh frowned. Hugh sighed.

"Your registration is expired."

"It is, Hugh, it is," I confessed for a second time as I clicked the ballpoint pen closed. "I am here to admit responsibility and to make it right. Hugh." I was trying to Hugh him into action.

"Where is your proof of insurance?" Hugh wondered.

I looked sinkingly down at the pile of papers Hugh held. And I had to admit the proof of insurance was not there. "It's out in the car, Hugh."

"Well." Hugh looked unsmiling into my face. "I gotta have your proof of insurance."

"So." I looked unsmiling into Hugh's face. "I need to go get it?"

"I gotta have your proof of insurance."

"Meaning I need to leave your window and go to my car and come back in and get into line ... all over again? Hugh?"

"I gotta have your proof of insurance."

The word "yes" didn't seem likely to rise from Hugh's DMV vocabulary. So I gathered my disappointing documents and turned away from Hugh and his hallowed window 6. I skulked out of the DMV to the parking lot, to my car, to the glove compartment, found the proof of insurance and ...

... returned to the nine-person line at the first-stop station in the DMV adventure. I received a new little printed ticket (M893), which I was instructed to take to the information station (stop 2), where sixteen people were ahead of me. When I finally reached her, the information lady was still rather nice and still smiling. She didn't remember me. Why would she? We had only had a brief "Ooo" encounter nearly two hours earlier. She examined my papers, uttered another "Ooo," summoned a new frown and—with her eyes—indicated the seating section with which I was woefully familiar.

I sat. I sighed. I noted the time (I had been there now a full two hours) and resumed reading Philip Levine's memories of jazz and poems in Detroit. My second visit to the time-stops-in-the-chairs-of-the-DMV waiting zone. I noticed others waiting. A variety of ages and hair colors. Earrings. Tattoos. Many sneakers. I don't wear sneakers. Sneakers always feel like you've given up on life. Even if you are young. If you're not wearing sneakers for sports, it seems to me there is only one reason to wear sneakers. For sneaking. I don't want to give up on life, and I don't want to sneak. So I don't wear sneakers. But there were many, many sneakers in the waiting area at the DMV. And a baby ... crying. She was wearing sneakers.

Philip Levine is good company, and I was soon happily lost again in his words. Then I worried that I might miss the loudspeaker calling my number. So I closed Philip Levine and listened to the crying baby. And watched the people waiting. And the people waiting on the people who had been waiting. Two and a half hours ground around. I felt like joining the baby in crying.

"M893, please go to window 11." Spoken loudly over the crying. And off to window 11 I went. I was greeted by Lula. As I plunked my papers on the desk in front of her, I noted that beside Lula's nameplate was another nameplate: "Trainee." That gave me a sinking feeling. Another in several sinking feelings I had experienced in my now two hours and forty-seven minutes. At the DMV.

Lula might have been new to her job; Lula might have been a "trainee," but Lula gave my documents a cursory examination, clicked her tongue, frowned and—without taking her gaze from my papers—intoned, "Your registration is expired." Though she was a DMV neophyte, she was sharp. But Lula's intoning was ominous.

"Yes, I know, Lula. It's why I'm here. Will you help me?" I presented the form Hugh had given me and that I had completed. She looked at it. She looked at my pile of papers (I swear they had begun to yellow. Like documents at the Smithsonian). "Look!" I urged Lula to look, "Here's my proof of insurance!" I was ashamed at the loudness of my eager hope that Lula would find me worthy.

"Hmm," Lula hmm-ed. I couldn't decipher her hmm. I could only read the context. And fill further with dread. I so hoped Hugh wasn't watching. "I've never handled this—I'm new to the job—so I will have to summon my supervisor."

"Oh," I oh-ed.

"Stanley!" Lula called from window 11 to wherever it is Stanley hangs out until he is needed. Stanley arrived. Frowning. He noticed I was clicking a DMV ballpoint pen nervously.

"Lula?" Stanley captured the "all" of the situation in merely uttering the trainee's name.

She explained my situation to the wrinkle-browed Stanley. He examined

32

my documents, looked at me, paused, and uttered, "Your registration is expired."

"It sure is, Stanley, it sure is," I agreed and wanted to add *and so is my patience with the charm of your goddamned DMV.*

Well, Lula and Stanley conferred in a DMV language of which I could catch only a few words: *insurance card, expired, form, no pen, sneakers.* Then Lula—with Stanley over her shoulder—clacked away on her computer. She looked at Stanley, he looked at the screen. He nodded, she clicked. I faded to invisibility as Lula and Stanley exchanged looks (and passed their meaningful time with technology) in the heart of the DMV. She asked. He answered. Lula jotted notes on a legal pad. Stanley nodded at her notes ... and came alarmingly DMV close to ... *smiling.*

The four-hour mark was approaching (the digital wall clock seemed to laugh at me) and I felt despair coming with it. Suddenly—from a Darth Vader distance—came a deep and foggy Stanley voice, proclaiming, "You're all set."

My knees threatened to collapse and I feebly responded, "Wh ... wh ... what?"

Lula leaped into my befuddlement, "You're all set."

My mood was beginning to shift from lost to giddy and I retorted, "I'm ... all ... set?"

Lula and Stanley answered in two-part harmony, "You're all set."

All that was left was to write a check to the DMV, gather my aging documents, and find a shred of dignity. I smiled a clumsy thank-you to Lula and Stanley, turned, and headed for the exit. I reached my car, started the engine, pulled out of the parking lot, and turned toward home. But as the DMV became smaller and smaller in my rearview mirror, a smugness rose in my chest because the joke was on Hugh and Lula and Stanley. I had committed a crime. In my pocket I carried away ... the DMV ballpoint pen.

Life and Poetry

It's odd how we end up with our jobs. Odd. Strange. Unplanned. For more than five decades I have been a broadcaster. Even during a four-year interruption for military service back in the 1960s I have been a broadcaster. Disc jockey. News reporter. Sports play-by-play and color commentator. I acted on the New York stage in *The Fantasticks, The Garden of Dromore, The Prince and the Pauper,* and a regional production of *Joseph and the Amazing Technicolor Dreamcoat.* And also appearances in a couple of films (*California Girls* and *Try to Remember*—a documentary about *The Fantasticks*). In 1971 I combed my hair, cinched up my tie, and walked across the hall from radio studio to television studio at KHQ in Spokane. I continued in radio as a disc jockey, but on the TV side I anchored the news, interviewed interesting (and boring) people, hosted a weekly children's talent show, and ... reported the weather.

I was never a good science student. I was never a good student of any kind in public school. When I was a boy south of Buffalo in Little Valley, New York, weather wasn't a science ... and it certainly wasn't a job. It was a playmate. Summer and the smell of clover on the hill, the hayfield ... green, then stubbly and brown after "haying." Thunderstorms scrubbed the sky to black iron and singed the air with lightning. Rain knocked down the grass. Weather wasn't a science. It was how autumn smoke from burning leaves stung your nose in days woven of a cooler thread. Weather certainly wasn't a science in winter—it was a co-conspirator speaking in the all-night wind whistling outside my bedroom that the coming blizzard would close school in the morning.

Then weather was spring and baseball and a throwing off of coats. It was a kiss or a kick or blessed swim, but never a science and certainly never a job. But when we went on the air in the summer of 1971 in Spokane at KHQ with a midday magazine program exotically called *The Noon Thing*, I was asked if I would add to my duties of host and interviewer on the program—the reporting of the weather. I humbly reminded the gathered folks that I knew nothing about the weather. The producer responded, "You don't need to. This is television." So. Having met the minimum requirement of knowing nothing about the subject, I became "the weatherman." An appellation I have come to despise.

Now, mind you I took the assignment seriously and studied the subject on the job. Over the years at various television stations I have picked up a worthy working knowledge of meteorology. And I have acquitted myself well enough to have earned my daily bread *often* as a weather reporter. But not *exclusively*.

As with you, I am not just a human *being*. I am a human *doing*. Doing and pursuing many activities that interest me—for pay, for pleasure. I have hosted a nightly magazine program on television. I've performed in commercials and films and "industrials" ("how to cook with a microwave," "how to dial a telephone"—honest). I have taught public speaking and creative writing (I hate *destructive* writing) and fiction and poetry in college. I have written columns for newspapers and magazines. I even have a couple of plays awaiting production. And casting. And financing.

One of my happiest writing pursuits was a monthly piece for *Spokane Magazine*. I was an essayist. And listed as a "contributing editor" on the masthead. That was perfect. Writing about anything that bubbled up in my mind or fluttered in front of my eyes. Playing on an aging softball team. Visiting a new and hip discotheque (as a decidedly *unhip* reporter). Riding on trains. Roaring with firefighters to a blaze. Impressions the month of February made on a third grader. All the while continuing to read ... *and write* poems.

I have always considered myself a performer, and I have acted in plays on the New York and New England stage for pay and fun. Or both. For many years I appeared as a dues-paying member of Actors' Equity in the long-running off-Broadway production *The Fantasticks*. I did several runs over a five-year period at the play's original home—the Sullivan Street Playhouse in Greenwich Village. I love *The Fantasticks* for its music, its story, its charm and ... its poetry. Early in 2018 I appeared as "Jacob" in *Joseph and the Amazing Technicolor Dreamcoat*. Jacob. Father of Israel. Not bad for a Methodist from Little Valley, New York. Great musical. Funny, poignant, smiling. And poetry.

Poetry is a handed-down tradition. Like fireworks. Or a parade. Like skipping a stone over a pond or kissing a girl under the pines behind the school at recess. As I imagine *you* did, *I* grew up with poetry. We enter and explore the meadows of poetry when we are young. The nursery rhyme. The song on the radio. The meadow of poetry is a lovely, exhilarating, laughing, weeping, frightening, silly, serious, sensuous place to be.

When I was in high school, a wisp of a teacher in a four-button suit assigned and read and talked about William Cullen Bryant and Walt Whitman and Henry Thoreau and Emily Dickinson and Robert Frost. *Frost*.

It was Robert Frost who guided me into the meadow of poems. Frost told me about a boy alone on his father's farm whose only play was what he could find himself, such as bending birch trees by climbing, then riding them down to the ground. That poem—what Richard Hugo calls "the trigger" for finding a subject, a muse—caught me and took me deeper and deeper into the meadow.

In 1964 I bought *The Road Not Taken*, a collection of Frost poems with critical and biographical commentary by Louis Untermeyer. The book pressed a pleasing green weight in my hand. A new book is always a thing that makes morning a particular joy to climb out of bed for. Suddenly that joy was shaped by Robert Frost. I still have that book from more than fifty years ago. It sits on a shelf in my study. It has traveled with me to a couple of colleges in New York. It has made trips with me to Texas. It has flown the Pacific for a two-year stay in Japan. That cherished book was with me for a decade in the evergreen state of Washington, then Ohio, and then New York. Now it lives with me here in Connecticut, absorbing the odor of nutmeg.

I open a book to go places old and shaded under drooping trees. Places peopled with farmers and wizards and kings and breathing women. Places of dogs and toads and wolves singing over the moonlit snow. Here. And on the other side of the earth.

A poem allows me to peer in on an old man grieving through a lonely night. A poem ushers me into the widow's heart ... to keep her secrets (or give them away when I loan the book that carries her story). A poem asks me to be a boy again, smiling at the thoughts and doings of the poem's boy. I want more than a mere *glimpse* of magic. The time in which we live deprives us because we never move slowly or stop ... *to see a thing longer.* This speeding century in which we live doesn't encourage us to go into poetry's meadow. One December day a few years ago a crystal cold descended on Connecticut, and as I drove into my town the sun threw ladder-rung shadows from the leafless trees across the road. My windshield flickered. The trees near a rock outcropping stood in the gray-brown shade of the hill. The trees farther out were still in sun, a scene to burn into the heart. But—driving—I zoomed past it all. That's how we live in this century. Only *glimpsing* magic. Never traveling slowly enough or stopping ... *to see a thing longer.* We don't go often enough into poetry's meadow. But it is so good to do so.

If ever there were a pursuit that ought to belong to the people, it is the poem. Ought to *belong* to the people. *Attract* the masses. Attract, inspire, delight. But some*where* some*one* some*time* in the long ago put the poem up on a high shelf misted from view. Only a privileged academician was interested enough to reach it. Only that person—the fellow with unkempt hair, wearing a sweater or the woman cradling books like a baby—climbed high enough upon their degrees and dusty theories to gain the shelf, to prick the mist, to own the poem.

A poem shouldn't sit far and dim and out of reach. Before it is darkened away into a book, it bubbles and fizzes with air and life. A poet isn't a theoretician. A poet isn't an out-of-touch scientist invoking lightning to strike life into fleshy thought in some spooky mountain castle. A poet is a noticer: how the wind slices into song at the corner of a house in winter; how green the baseball field was when first seen framed in the stadium entry arch. A poet notices how big a spring creek *sounds* and how small it *looks* when summer sucks its water up into the hot, hanging air. A kiss in a corridor. Rain on the window of a train. Sunlight bouncing secondhand from a glass skyscraper down to the street. A poet notices the small breeze when someone—out of view—opens the door to the room where he sits. The poet notices the arch of an eyebrow in a conversation to which he is invited, or only eavesdropping on.

And a poem itself is a butterfly. Hard to catch but, once caught, easy to hold for its rhythm and rhyme. And the poem is worth seeing longer. A poem—like sleepiness and imaginings—turns clouds into uncharted continents and gives the very night, itself, a soul.

No matter how we crank our days to table our bread or to pay for the roof above it; no matter whether our automobile is leased or bought or used; no matter if church is where we go to rub God's elbow or because it's a sweet stone sight against the sky, we're all poets. And to have our natural, native love of verse bored out of us by dulled teaching, or shamed into a dark corner of our mind, is wrong. A poem is a song to sing. A song for *all* to sing.

A poem, as I said, is a butterfly. But not to be caught and killed and carved. A poem is a joy, a pang, a hope, a hate, a second, a century, a drink, a feast, a villain, a kiss, a curse, a love, a loss, a time. And like air and dignity, it belongs to us all. We all deserve the poem because it is alive, fluttering, colored and sweet. Or dark. But we all have it. It's right that we have it. It's good that we have it. The life of the soul demands it.

Flipping Over a Whig

I happened on a photograph of Princeton's restored Whig Hall. *Nice* in a comforting, old-fashioned niceness. In so many senses. But ah, the classical design of the building. The sturdy stone walls, the tall, proud columns. A design of nineteenth-century architect A. Page Brown. The building's name: Whig Hall. *Whig?* That made me stroke my chin to feel if any Lincolnesque whiskers had sprouted. Well, whiskers *were* sprouted and, in truth, I had more than a single chin to check, but the word "Whig" conjured sepia scenes of waistcoats and asymmetrical bow ties and grim countenances. Nobody smiled in the nineteenth century. Whigs nor Democrats nor Secessionists. I read somewhere that there were no "say cheese" grins in photos from those days because you had to hold really still for several seconds so that Mathew Brady could capture your image with his new, slow, bulky camera. It's hard to hold a smile for several seconds. Unless you have just won the lottery or you're petting a puppy. Apparently there were no lotteries or puppies back in the 1800s. Only poker and really serious adult dogs. In pictures from back then nobody is smiling. Or shaving.

But in this photograph Whig Hall looks like its doors have just clanked closed on frock coats or hoopskirts or bonnets with their wearers getting ready for a debate or a Chautauqua lecture. It was (it *is* ...) home to the Whig-Cliosophic Society. Great name, eh? "Cliosophic." A neologism coined by long-ago New Jersey governor (and Princeton alumnus) William Paterson. He assigned it the meaning "in praise of wisdom." The photo looks black-and-white even though the beautiful building is beige against a bright blue sky. And built of what? Marble? Granite? How were the bulky pieces transported from where to there? It's a classical Greek Ionic structure. I looked it up. (It's good to have such words as *cliosophic* and *ionic* bubbling and fizzing—like leftover turkey alchemizing into soup—in one's vocabulary vat.)

I gaze at the photograph. The bare branches of the leaning, listening trees seem rooted in those gone-away days. No leaves. I guess leaves—like lotteries and puppies—had not been invented yet, either. Any suggestion of movement in the photograph of this solid, stolid structure comes from the shadows of the trees. It seems a wind is moving through them, whispering windy words. I think of Keats's "Ode on a Grecian Urn," where he addresses wedding revelers forever frozen with "Thou foster-child of Silence and slow Time." Whig Hall is forever frozen, too. Frozen but warm. And another sound playing on my mind's ear is how Whig Hall's early audiences were summoned to the lecture, to the debate. Perhaps (thank you, again, Mr. Keats) with "pipes and timbrels"? Whig Hall goes back to 1895. And its walls and floors tattoo with the sounds of boots and hoots and huzzahs.

I love the photograph of this magnificent old building. No matter how modern it is—with new "fire-code specifications," "accessibility improve-ments," and "egress path upgrades"—Whig Hall is a comforting reminder of a time we know only from fuzzy images and how that word—*image*—is still the root and fuel of its sibling word ... *imagination.* I'd like to step into Whig Hall and try to hear the oratory ... in praise of wisdom.

III

The Sun and Returns

Solar Savings

Kathleen Vick stirred my thinking in an *OfficeInsight* article, "Putting My Money Where My Mouth Is." Great research. Great spirit. I applaud such thinking ... and planning and calculating and determining and measuring and consulting and specifying and marking and installing and inspiring. Why has it taken so long for us as a people to consider how to lasso light to enhance our lives? Rather than just allowing it to soften the M&M's left on the passenger seat of my 1938 Ferblungeon?

The sun has been hanging in the sky for ... well, I can't say how long, but I'll bet it's been there for years. My house is surrounded by trees. Mostly maples, but there is one sprawling and shaggy pine that starts on a front corner and bends around to the side and overhangs the deck. I love this tree. It is large and scruffy. But the wind through its needles and boughs is as sweet as a symphony. And the sunlight through those needles and boughs is absolutely spiritual. There comes one of those exquisitely precious moments in summer as evening starts to slowly close the lid on the day by slipping the sun down behind the trees-y hill across the street. That sun alchemizes the soft needles from green to gold. It is a moment when the wind pauses and the birds are mute. If I am there to see it and alone, this leaving light from the sun graces my solitude. It is possible for this leaving light to lift me out of unhappinesses and disappointments. In that moment.

The light borrows some*thing* from some*where*. This light, this leaving sunlight, has visited another and unearthly place and has gathered magic or smiling or purity from that other place before coming to my pine needles to give the yawning day a simple beauty. This gift is given to my pine. It's given to a pond in the woods. To leaves hanging over the street. It's given to grass waving in a meadow. To the fluttering wings of birds. To clouds clumping in the smooth blue sky planning their mischief of thunder and rain.

Now, the sun offers the gift of warming and lighting and powering your house and mine. My regard of our nearest simmering star has usually been more prosaic. When I was a boy, early in summer vacation, my mother would write my name in lipstick on my back and send me into the baking outdoors. To play baseball or catch; to swim or hike up the little hill behind our house; or to wade in the creek which juddered beside the lawn. A couple of afternoon hours was all it took for my skin to tan. Everywhere but where the lipstick spelled my name. (There was, often in summer, not much to do in my little hometown. My parents enjoyed watching bowling on television because of the penmanship of the guy who kept score. So it was only fitting that my mom would write my name on my back and let the sun do the rest.) It wasn't a wise activity, given all we know now, about the dangers of prolonged exposure to the rays of the sun. But remember, this was back in the days when the prevailing notion of caution and good sense was waiting one hour after a meal before going swimming.

The sun was always there. To greet me in the morning and follow me on my bike as I pedaled through the streets of town. It bathed the baseball field. Lured the clover up out of the ground. Made you wish you hadn't worn shorts when you slid onto the plastic seat in your buddy Boober's dad's Buick. Ouch. The sun made shade a destination. It grew corn and beans. It browned the lawn. It made a beagle sleepy. When the sun was up it was always up to something. Displaying a mother's penmanship or showing you which rows in the garden needed weeding. It's always there. Even on a cloudy day. Even on the cloudiest day. The sun is simply, always, flaringly ... *there.* On those days, it may not be *sun*light; but, it is *day*light and we have the sun to thank. Or, now ... to capture, to harness. To draw into partnership. And Kathleen Vick has "shed light" on how to do this.

I like the lingo: "photovoltaic cells." Sounds like a place one would put a Martian convicted of some felony in a '50s movie. And "grid" and "gratis." A couple of great words. Alliterative. Thriftily syllabled. "Grid" sounds like it just tumbled out of ESPN. And "gratis"? Who doesn't like that word? Think of it applied to theater tickets or French fries. There are the "Kyocera PV modules" or "inverter." I don't have any idea what they are, but I want some. Then there is that thing labeled "Fronius IG" in a photo. I envy the person having one of those. You take people down into the basement and they see that hanging on the wall and utter a quiet, "Ahhh." And you respond, "Yep. It's a Fronius."

Of course, in the middle of her first paragraph, Kathleen writes about her and her husband "rid[ing] off into the sunset." With so much invested in solar energy and that Fronius IG, she'd better aim for "riding off into the sun-*rise*." About the only energy in the dark are here-and-there fireflies. And they don't really do much. Even if you catch them and put them into a jelly jar.

A Brief Visit

Coming back ... to Spokane. Those were my thoughts as March approached. *This* time I hoped to be smiling. The *last* time I viewed Spokane was through tears. For the second time in my life. I learned how it is to leave a place I love. I had only a month to accustom myself to the idea of leaving Spokane and my life at KHQ. Then on a sunny July Monday, I just walked out of the house and into my auto ... and drove away. The lanes on I-90 leading out of my home of ten years were a press of workbound traffic. There was plenty of room in the lanes leading to Idaho. I *needed* plenty of room. It's hard to steer a Dodge when you're crying.

I regained my composure by Post Falls. I had to. I didn't want to motor through Coeur d'Alene with oncoming traffic seeing me crying. And risk it thinking I was a wimp.

Driving out of my Spokane decade, there were memories packed in my heart like the luggage packed in my car (but the memories didn't have dippy little stickers from Disneyland or Carlsbad Caverns on them).

From Spokane to Cincinnati; 2,100 miles. By automobile. My father came along for the ride, and we were joined by my little dog Burfie, who we had to sneak into motels along the way (and we were successful, until one Holiday Inn in Indiana).

I've crossed the country several times by train. I knew the size of the undertaking. From craggy, lovely Idaho, we moved at 60 miles per hour into craggy, lovely western Montana. I make the distinction between *western* and *eastern* here because *eastern* Montana has only "craggy" going for it. The ground rises high over the little pockets of humanity in eastern Montana.

46

I liked the small buildings at the base of a mountain looking even smaller because of the mountain. For all our accomplishments in technology and architecture, with all our Empire State Buildings and jumbo jets, we need only see the rippled tin roof of a wooden shack squatting beneath a Montana mountain to yank us back to cosmic humility.

As we zoomed along the good concrete highway, I grew aware of a thinning of trees. The same sort of dwindling forestry I'd pondered at the fringes of Cheney, Washington, countless times. The rocks and brown grass grew in my view as the trees sputtered to nearly nothing. When the land threw off the last of its evergreens, I knew we'd reached Montana's eastern half. Here folks have been dressing like John Wayne longer than John Wayne dressed like John Wayne. I saw so many horses and cows that I had to watch where I stepped at the rest stops.

Ditto North Dakota. Minnesota arrived just in time to save us, because the Dakota countryside had me just one barren lull away from sleep. In Minnesota, it's back to the business of forests and lakes and rolling hills. A place summer is kind to. A place that takes the gold of the sun and weaves it with intense shades of green—grass, trees, ferns, fields, farms, meadows. As we worked our way farther and my eyes grew accustomed to scenery again, I saw a road sign announcing the approach of Sauk Centre. Sauk Centre? Why did that name mean something to me? Where had I heard it? Sauk Centre. As the little village rose into view, another sign answered my question: "Sinclair Lewis Avenue, Next Right." Sinclair Lewis! *Main Street! Babbitt! Arrowsmith!*

The Nobel Prize (Lewis was the first American to win it for literature). We entered the still small and sleepy village. It was much as it must have been when Lewis was a boy there, growing up in a Victorian frame house with a sprawling lawn and looming shade trees. Sinclair Lewis's home. I stood looking at the old house, trying to imagine the young Sinclair absorbing the characters and images of this little American town that would haunt the world and the readers of good books.

Another sign on a post on Main Street declared this was "the original Main Street." My joy at being near the mystic stirrings of literary greatness was attended by a touch of wonder at the local people taking a dubious pride in Lewis, oblivious to the irony, not seeing the banality of their attempts to turn creative genius into a tourist attraction.

Back on the interstate we roared away from the past and back to the present as we headed toward Wisconsin. That state looks as though it were magically snatched from New England. Stone fences. Woods. Dairy herds. Cozy farms. And flashing blue police lights. Police lights? Oh, no. In the bright morning sunshine condensed in my rearview mirror I saw an officer waving me to the side of the road: 68 in a 55 mph zone.

I confess to taking a perverse pleasure in my crime. I take such poor care of an automobile that it would be challenged to even exceed a school-zone speed limit. The officer was really quite pleasant, and after giving me the citation he asked which was more unpopular in the state of Washington—Mount St. Helens or the governor.

We were back on the road and slipping from river-splashed Wisconsin into flat-iron Illinois, quickly shifting from prairie to city as we slipped into Chicago. That toddlin' town. Gateway to the American West. "Tool Maker." "Stacker of Wheat." "Player with Railroads." (Thank you, Carl Sandburg.) Sears Tower. The Loop. The Cubs and the White Sox and da Bears. Saul Bellow. Al Capone. Traffic jams. We missed all of that. Except the traffic jams.

July in Chicago is not a month. It's a threat. It weaves the fragrances wafting out of the stockyards and the belching of the nearby steel mills to lower the charm of summer. Add heavy traffic to the mix and you begin to question the wisdom of Henry Ford and his assembly line.

We snailed along in ninety-degree heat a mere three miles in two and a half hours. We joined the similarly inching-along humanity confined between the dotted lines. July heat. Gasoline fumes. Diesel fumes. The grinding groan of trucks. Smoke and dust and damnation. Then a gradual acceleration ... 20, 30, 35, 45, and finally 55 miles per hour. We were back to motoring. Gliding past the Chicago lakefront, with the acrid breeze even feeling good. We slipped into yellow, hazy, industrial Indiana.

Then a veer south and away from windy city heat. Though flat as a writer's wallet, Indiana is a visual joy of tree-carpeted farms and villages. After a few hours we reached Indianapolis, skirted it, and swung east with our destination nearly in view.

We knew Indiana was about to become Ohio when the land began to rise and gently fall and give our road some curves. I saw the Ohio River, wide and winding and speckled with little shards of sun. And the skyline of Cincinnati welcomed me to my new home. All my thoughts were borne to my consciousness on cherished thoughts of other places I have loved.

After we had settled into our new home, one day I lay on the grass of a little rounded Cincinnati hill. A time-honored thought came. The sun *I* see here is the same sun *you* see in Spokane and Connecticut and Little Valley. The sunlight caught the top of the hill and the grass. The summer yellow-green was enough to melt away, for that summer moment, the miles between you—and me. Then I heard a volleyball game and a wife asking her husband if the burgers were done. I heard a small airplane puttling overhead, trailing a sign that congratulated someone named Harry. I rose from the ground and thought about heading home. And I remembered I was already there ... in Ohio.

IV

Pens and Dogs and Jam

Penned In

I am fond of ballpoint pens. *Too* fond, I fear. I buy them by the box at a big store. One of those gigantic cement-floored, tall-ceilinged, warehouse-y, airplane hangar-y, parking-lot-clotted, mega-membership outfits where your picture is stamped on a plastic card so you can stuff it into your wallet already bulging with so many other plastic cards there is no room for money. I rarely shop there. Once every couple of years. But when I go there, I buy ballpoint pens. And a jar of cashews. Pens and nuts are sold in such volume that I only need to shop there every couple of years.

The pens are the same. Always. Blue plastic. With a matching blue cap that features a clip for the shirt pocket where the pen (and its boxed fellows) will spend its cursive life. Blue ink. Medium point. I love that pen. I love the whole huge boxful. I have two book bags. My father's generation called a book bag a *briefcase*. My father wasn't a lawyer, he was a blacksmith. And never owned a briefcase that I can remember, but he knew what one was. And it wasn't a book bag. But mine is. And I have two. One is black. The other is green canvas. Each has zippers and pockets. And pockets with zippers. Great repositories for fistfuls of blue ballpoint pens. I never leave home without one pen in my pocket and hundreds in the zippered pockets of my two book bags. Of course, there are *books* in my book bags, but fewer—because of their bulk—than ballpoint pens.

So, I have ballpoint pens in boxes, in drawers, in a little pewter cup sitting colonially on my desk. There are ballpoint pens on my nightstand, on my dresser, beside my triple-A-battery-powered clock that sits on the counter of my bathroom sink. When my shirts and trousers return from the cleaners there is always a little plastic bag with two or twenty ballpoint pens that a nice dry-cleaner guy captured before they did whatever they do to my shirts and trousers. The pen always finds its way home. Which makes it odd that I become upset when I lose one. *Vaguely* upset. But upset.

There are blue-ink ballpoint pens in the glove box of my 1938 Ferblungeon. In the little elastic pockets behind the driver *and* passenger seats. I visit the car wash even less often than I visit the store where I buy boxes of pens, but when I do, when I am shamed—at the risk of tetanus from my car's fusty, dusty, musty, crusty interior—to motor to the car wash (which I seldom visit because there are too many choices for cleaning and waxing and deodorizing and undercoating and buffing and burnishing), the fellows who do the interior find a pen or six. When I go to the hose-it-yourself-cheapo-sudser, I always recover some. (You should see how the preceding sentence looks on notebook paper, in blue ink, in cursive. Sweet.) I find ballpoint pens in our clothes washer after the spin cycle has spun. And sometimes they're in the dryer's lint trap.

The pens have plinged out from beneath the graggling lawn mower like tiny Smurf ballistic missiles. Ball*point*-istic missiles. My little dog Lily has found them buried with bones, with chewed tennis balls, and beside the morning paper. It's as if they have something to add.

I have loaned them to my children, but they understand they must come back. The pens, I mean. Pens don't grow on trees. They come blue and medium-pointed and capped in bulging boxes from a store big enough to have its own UN ambassador. And I am fond of them. *Too* fond, I fear. Fond of the ballpoint pen. And cashews.

Collies and Wallys and Making Scents

Thumbing through the September 8 *OfficeInsight* was a particular pleasure (though the thumb is not a practical tool in reading an online publication). I love dogs. And the photo of Moses on page 6 charmed me. He's the bearded collie of a fellow named Paul, a labor negotiator, a six-foot-ten-inch labor negotiator. I imagine Paul prevails in plenty of the negotiations. *Sitting*, he's taller than I am. There was no mention in the caption of Moses's height. The dog in my life is Wally. He is constructed like me. Chubby with short legs. Those legs churn a blurry churn when fetching a tennis ball, but they're short, like mine, which is just fine with Wally and me. Moses caught my eye. Then an article caught my nostrils.

Scrolling on to page 14, I learned that a seminar on scents was held September 25. The article claims the scent industry was begun in 1190. Probably because showers, Dial soap, and Speedstick were still centuries away. 1190? There had to be some serious hygiene issues. No at-the-strip-mall pharmacy for popping in and picking up a gourd of Head-and-Haunches dandruff shampoo. Can you imagine a twelfth-century Indian summer afternoon following a spirited few innings of Wiffle ball? There had to be serious thought, some passionate chat about the pressing need for shower stalls and spray cologne. There must have been wrinkled noses in the crowd around the postgame wagon-gate grill party. ("Dude. Go chill on the other side of the leafy glen, will ya? Whew.") Apparently scent consulting does business to an annual tune of eighteen billion dollars. That doesn't stink. It does mean it is really a nascent industry. There will be a seminar at Sheridan College. Who'd have thought such a thing back in gamy 1190? I'm only on the periphery of the industry. I have a candle whose aroma is orange and cinnamon. I usually light it when Wally scrabbles in from a game of fetch. Or a sudden rain. That's about as therapeutic as my fragrances get. But I'd love to go to Sheridan College to learn more. Do they allow dogs on campus?

Canada has had a busy September ... with the seminar on scents and now Toronto is discussing *nothing*. Really. Toronto is a great city. Hemingway called it home in the 1920s and wrote some sinewy prose for the *Toronto Star*. Then there *was* Robertson Davies and there *is* Margaret Atwood. When I spent a few days there back in the late '90s, I reveled in all the Toronto brick and literature and a baseball park (whose roof opens and closes ... like a Batmobile). Well, days ago, a panel got together to consider "Unbuilt Toronto: Visions of the Toronto that Could Have Been, through Projects That Never Were." Sounds like a Robertson Davies title, right there. It's "back to the drawing board" not for correction, but for noting empty air. With perhaps a little regret? Architects and historians will reconsider buildings and highways and whole neighborhoods that never moved beyond being good ideas. Well, as I have always said, "You can bore a tunnel, but you must never bore a panel member."

And I liked the latest installment of Kathleen Vick's mission of greening her home and life. Her earlier-mentioned solar panels are wonderful. A bright idea in every sense. Or scents (to stay with our theme). Now it's on to water treatment. I've always favored treating water better. Well, Kathleen has added to her quest some "Watts sediment filters and charcoal filters" in a gray, bulbous piece of equipment called "Big Bubba." She's installed the solar panels, the water PEX system, and heck, she has even consulted with the "Rheem rep" (which sounds more ominous than environmental). But "Big Bubba"? Big Bubba. More than good for kindly treating your water, Big Bubba is something even Wally and Moses might enjoy. Or fetch.

Grocery Jam

The bar code. I was impressed. Leaning on my cart in the express line at my neighborhood Whip-In-Check-Out supermarket, I was well below the twelve or fewer requirement. I had nine items sitting on the conveyer belt. Feeling smug and mellow. The burly checker wore a scruffy beard and an I-can't-wait-for-five-o'clock countenance. I counted again. Nine items. The limit was twelve. I was golden.

But suddenly, the woman in front of me encountered some sort of glitch in her transaction. A *delaying* glitch. More than twelve items? Scanner couldn't read her credit card? Or was it a debit card? I don't know. I looked away as we are wont to do when pretending that a child is not having a tantrum or there is tomato sauce on the cheek of the stranger asking directions.

The checker had briskly swiped all of her items through the doomaflahjee that reads the bar code and the total toted up and away. The bar code was plinking along coding or decoding or barring or debarring or whatever in heck it is the bar code does. It was doing it really well. It uttered its chirpy little punctuation to each proffered product as my nine items flonked along the counter, queuing up waiting to take the cue for their own scans. The express line is a blessing. Until it stalls.

I waited. Hands clamping more tightly on shopping cart. Briefly entranced by the ad—on the seat of the cart—for a friendly-looking real estate agent named Burt. Great teeth. Spiffy hair. And the best houses (make that *homes*) found in town. The delay ahead continued. I pondered ecology and global warming and rehearsed my response to "Paper or plastic?" It'd be paper. My mellowed smugness heightened. My attention slipped from the real estate guy to the last-chance-for-candy shelf beside my idled cart. Wow. Chocolate-covered pretzels. Soft-baked cookies—two of them—in a bright plastic wrapper. Applesauce in a tube. *Applesauce in a tube?* What an idea. How innovative. Just thinking about downing applesauce from a tube made me feel like an astronaut.

The express jam was still at *full* jam when my gaze swung left to the magazines. And the woe befalling famous people. Past affairs coming to light. Rude treatment by devoted fans. Intriguing relationships with creatures from places far beyond earth. All of the famous faces in the photos were downhearted. They looked drawn and tense and troubled. And I thought, "Gee. If only they sold real estate they wouldn't be sad. They'd be happy like Burt."

My reverie took me back to the little three-aisle grocery in my hometown of Little Valley where I briefly worked when I was sixteen. No bar codes back then. I had to ring up the purchases on the old *sh-shunk* cash register. And return the change by working it out in my head, which caused me to wish I had *really* paid attention to arithmetic in the third grade. And how I wished I understood how to remove only the *browning* leaves from the lettuce heads. Because when I was finished, the lettuce heads looked like Brussels sprouts. The boss was so annoyed that he banished me to the cellar to sort soda bottles draped in cobwebs. My brother Harlow had worked in that little store four years before I had. He was gifted and efficient. I was neither. Five years after Harlow moved on from groceries to college, he was elected—*on the first ballot*—to the Grocery Hall of Fame. I was so inept I was sent down to the minors. Or to the cellar, actually. To sort soda bottles. And I was never called up again.

Then the express line lurched back to life. The lady ahead was rolling out of the aisle with her bagged and over-the-limit groceries. I was back in the nine-item present where soda bottles are plastic, where applesauce comes in a tube, and where there are no cobwebs anywhere in the world. All thanks to the bar code.

V

Nowadays and Then-adays

Signing On

Archeologists make a big deal about cave paintings. Thousands of years ago, the tales of the tribe were dabbed on the dark, smoke-smudged walls. There was no *written* language. It was all pictures. Wooly mammoth. Shaggy Bob, who lived one stalagmite over and had a role in the inventing of the wheel. The occasional pterodactyl, a here-and-there eucalyptus tree. Nowadays we know about then-adays from the sketchers whose canvas was the interior of a drafty, rocky cavern-sweet-cavern.

We were driving around northern Vermont a few days ago. Winter was still full-blown winter and not just a claim on the calendar. Snow lay deep in the meadows and white through the trees. Plows had turned the sides of the roads into a lumpy rubble. It was the *sides* of those roads, also, that caught my attention. Highway signs. You know ... the yellow diamonds warning of what might be ahead. And I realized we still tell tales with pictures.

In northern Vermont there is the sign with a silhouetted moose. And it's a worthy warning. A moose is big and substantial. A moose can weigh as much as a car; a collision can be dramatic. And dangerous. But the black moose on the highway sign is impressive, statu*esque* and statue-*like*. Not cute like the leaping deer or the soporific cow alerting you to the cow crossing just ahead. (I would've thought the cow could infuse her sign with a little action. Especially since it warns of the cow *doing* something. In this case *plodding* ... across the road. But the sign has the cow simply standing there. Udderly *unmoving*.) The moose looks like he could graciously adorn a park or a battlefield. If a moose, rather than a horse, had been pressed into the service of carrying a soldier from the tent to the front, that'd make a memorable shrine.

Experts allude to the "primitiveness" of cave paintings. The anatomies of the humans and the beasts are inaccurate, distorted, their depictions the inchoate stirrings of an artistic sensibility on its way but, still far from artistry. Well ... what about the roundheaded bald pedestrian featured on *today's* signs? He has no hands nor feet. I must say *that's* pretty primitive. He's leaning as if his back hurts. Sometimes he clumps through two parallel lines which suggest a crosswalk, and sometimes he is just floating—in his painful posture—in the yellow-diamond air. Does that mean he is crossing the road ahead or just meandering in the meadow? I say give the guy some context. And feet.

There was a time when the story was told in words. "Dead End." "Stop Ahead." "One Lane Bridge." "Bump." "Hill." And the vaguely arousing "Soft Shoulder." That one always conjured thoughts of assignations, not loose gravel. On still other signs, you'd be alerted to the impending ending of lanes—left and right. A road narrowed, a bridge narrowed. I love "Dip." Shelly took a photo of me standing by a "Dip" sign in rural Kentucky back in the '80s. I still have the photo. And I still am a dip.

Back then, the signs were a literature of words ... to be *read*. Now, alas, they're cave paintings again. A truck on a yellow triangle. A riderless bicycle on a yellow triangle. An unremarkable farmer on an unremarkable tractor. A car on a pair of squiggly lines. Or the roundheaded fellow atop a snowmobile (with a gray hinge across the snowmobile that allows you to fold up the sign for a couple of weeks in the northern Vermont summer). But enough. I must close here. Time to start cooking dinner. On this new thing the neighbors call "fire."

VI

Training, Timing, and Morphological Musings

Wide and Wavy Out of Salamanca

When we got married back in 1944
  We'd board that Silverliner below Baltimore
  Tripped to Virginia on a sunny honeymoon
  Nobody cares about the railroads anymore

We'd tip that porter for a place of our own
  Then send a postcard to your Mom and Dad back home
  Did somethin' to ya when you'd hear that "All aboard"
  Nobody cares about the railroads anymore

We had a daughter and you oughta see her now
  She has a boyfriend who looks just like My Gal Sal
  And when they're married they won't need us anymore
  They'll board an aeroplane and fly away from Baltimore

Did somethin' to ya when you'd hear that "All aboard"
  Nobody cares about the railroads anymore

—Harry Nilsson, "Nobody Cares about the Railroads Anymore"

I was on an Erie Lackawanna Railroad coach moving wide and wavy out of the Salamanca, New York, station bound for Olean—twenty-five miles distant—and a tour of a bakery. My fellow second graders and I had waited impatiently in front of the red-brick station for our first ride on this most magical, most urbane, most inviting mode of people-transports.

"Don't step over that white line!" a seasoned second grader had warned our small group, "or the train'll suck you right into 'er wheels!" A shudder ran the route of my suspenders.

A train big enough to snatch a seven-year-old off his feet was ambling into view. Then, with a fingernail-on-chalkboard squeal, the metal giant sighed to a stop. Thirty pairs of little eyes widened in the blue shadow. Steam licked out from under the engine. Our boarding platform filled with people—conductors, porters, baggagemen, travelers, engineers, mechanics, brakemen.

This train gave me a ride like none I had ever taken. Nothing like the ride in my dad's Oldsmobile. Or the handlebar of my brother Harlow's three-speed Hercules Genuine English bicycle. Certainly this train was in a different league completely from my own wrinkled and rusty Radio Flyer wagon.

This train was huge. Heavy. It had seats facing ... backward. It had a drinking fountain, a bathroom. *Seats ... facing ... backward!* With little doilies. I tried to imagine doilies in Dad's Oldsmobile. This train was the biggest, strongest, fanciest mechanical creature I'd ever had the delirious good fortune to encounter. This was living. It beat playing Red Rover. It beat kickball. This twenty-mile train ride beat my Gabby Hayes frontier tent. My Superman comic book collection. And it sure as the dickens beat the bakery it was carrying us to.

Since that long-ago journey, I've crossed America some twenty times. From west to east; north to south and back. Once in the late 1960s I ventured from New York to Chicago, then veered down into Texas on the *Super Chief.* My memories of travel reverberate with the sounds of hissing brakes, creaking metal, a fast-passed crossing bell, the hushed, sleepy talk of night riders, and the click of the conductor's ticket punch. And the everyday noises that mingle with the constant murmur of a train on the rails: the rattle and clink of the dinner hour, an electric razor, an unfolding newspaper, the splashing sink. These sounds underlined by the steady, muffled music of speeding on steel. Traveling by train, I find life still spends its time as it always has, but in a dimension zipping at 70 miles an hour. I've ridden trains through America, subways in New York and Boston and Washington and Toronto, the Elevated over Chicago, a monorail in Seattle, and a swift, sleek electric in Japan. And every time I'm train traveling, a pleasant tremble fills my being, fills my journey.

Railroading has been written about, talked about, filmed, painted, photographed, and pondered. A map of the country's trains—freight and passenger—resembles the blood vessels of the human body. Taking life to the nation's extremities. *Life. Feeling.* Sustaining, replenishing, vitalizing. It was the railroad that took people to the cities and cities to the people. The railroads carved a trough across the continent. Lining that trough was a tube. Inside that tube was a grace untouched by time. Fine silverware and china. Impeccably uniformed men attending to each traveler's each whim. Huge seats beside huge windows through which to marvel at a nation wide open and tree-carpeted or a nation dusted with the shabbiness of tumbling-down cities or a nation of horizon-reaching prairies dotted with sagebrush and cattle skulls. The train showed it all, took us through it all. And to it all.

Here I close my eyes and sigh: *an old Burlington Northern passenger train rattles west through Wisconsin. The moon keeps pace just beyond a black and ragged line of trees. I've been watching that moon for some time, a neglected book lies open on my lap. My military uniform announces that I am not on vacation. I'm on my way to a new assignment, and this great, swaying train is my way to get there. We've all heard the distant train whistle in the night. That whistle weaves with enviable stealth from our subconsciousness to our consciousness ... and back. I can only recall that sound when I am actually* hearing it.

Ah ... trains and train stations. Boarding announcements echoing off marble walls. Tickets checked and frayed from frequent handling. Increasingly wrinkled clothes worn in waking hours and in sleep.

"I'll have a hamburger and soda, please." The waiter takes my order in the lurching dining car. In the mirror along one wall I see a tiny white-haired woman sitting near me. The waiter turns to her and she orders, "Three hamburgers and a

piece of apple pie, please."

Where's she going to put it, I wonder. She can't weigh a hundred pounds. I return to my face in the mirror. Circles darken beneath my eyes. Not just tired. Lonely. Lonely and homesick. Homesick and unhappy. And with every minute I'm a mile farther from home. So damned sad.

The hamburgers arrive in front of the old woman and me at the same time. I start my solitary meal—preoccupied with the ebb of my emotions. A sudden, gentle tug at my sleeve brings me back to the train hurtling with the moon through the Wisconsin countryside.

"Young man, excuse me." The woman stares seriously. "I'm afraid I'm not as hungry as I thought. Will you help me?

She pushes two hamburgers toward me on the counter. Then the apple pie.

"My grandson is in the military, too."

My cheeks grow warm. I thank her. She simply smiles, pays both of our checks, and in the unsteady dining car unsteadily walks away. Suddenly my train ride is an adventure again. And if I'm not with loved ones, I am, at least, near a loving one. Someone who matters. Someone who makes me feel that I matter, too.

My generation has slipped easily into the past tense when talk turns to trains. There's still a generation for whom the railroad industry lives in gilded memory as a noisy, throbbing, treasured piece of life. Railroading *was* a life ... to be lived—the shrill whistle, the groan of the engine rolling away from the station, the fluid ride through the night, sunlight flickering from car to car under a western sky that starts but never stops.

One evening a few autumns ago, rain was beating a locomotive rhythm on the shingles of a South Hill home in Spokane (where I lived at the time). The house belonged to a fellow named Walt. I was there to chat with him and his friend Tom. Both retired from a life of working on the railroad. They invited me to sit in on their memories.

Walt grew up in Helena, Montana, early in the twentieth century. After roughing it with a surveying gang, he stepped into the world of trains. This was back in the Roaring Twenties (when trains did their share of the roaring). He left the surveying job when his gaze fell upon the misty Cascade Mountains—that giant spine of earth, rock, and trees that has inspired the artist and confounded the traveler—in western Washington. Walt was hired to join the task of cutting a tunnel through those Cascades.

"I don't like to work underground," Walt declared upon arriving at the site. Half an hour later he had a job, which soon took him six miles into the dark earth. At the end of every day Walt would come back to the pine-scented surface. And promptly quit. Fully determined to never go back into that tunnel. And every next morning, he was back. Back in the tunnel. The pay was good. And, well, *somebody* had to transform those mountains from barriers to rail routes to scenery. Walt was one of those somebodies. And the line from Spokane to points west to Seattle became a straighter, shorter one.

Even so utilitarian a thing as a tunnel can be a wonderful experience on a train. I'm not talking about New York's Lincoln Tunnel or the Holland Tunnel. Their rows of fluorescent lights along the walls and ceilings bathe the entire route with a kind of "mother's kitchen" glow. Familiar. Ordinary. Unremarkable. A railroad tunnel, though—to the unsuspecting passenger—is a sudden plunge into night, a cowl thrown over the day. One minute you're watching the land zipping by, and the next you're looking back at yourself in a window-suddenly-turned-mirror.

There's a tunnel in the Sierra Nevadas I'll always remember. Those mountains rear up in Nevada and don't slip back down until they're in California. I was on a train one sunny April afternoon, looking out at an America that was wild and wondrous. The train slowed as it moved onto a precarious track along one of the many cliffs. My heart quickened as I peered a thousand feet down at the forest below. I rose from my seat to move to the other side of the coach—my acrophobia (why I travel by train in the first place) was subduing my love of beautiful scenery. I was wobbly crossing the aisle as we whisked into a tunnel. And darkness. But I was exhaling in relief at being surrounded by a mountain. When we emerged from the tunnel, the track was bordered on both sides by bulging mounds of earth, and we moved steadily—happily—ever downward and nearer to sea level.

I lifted from my reverie here to the sound of the deep, rich voice of Walt's friend, six-foot-four-inch Tom from Dunseith, North Dakota. Tom looked like a motion-picture cowboy, but his heart belonged to the mighty steel road of our three-way reminiscing. Tom's papa was a railroad man. His son still is. At one point grandfather, son, and grandson worked for the Great Northern at the same time. Three generations of railroad men. The same might happen in banking or meat cutting, but not with the charm and adventure.

Tom's one of the best talkers of railroading legend I've ever heard. When railroad men get together, "Oh, I tell ya," Tom tells ya, "the cinders fly!" Tom leaned forward in his chair. "It's just like baseball. The longer it's been since I've played, the better I get! The same thing with railroading."

That took Walt back to 1949, when he was in a three-man crew inspecting bridges between Everett and Wenatchee. The crew was doing its work traveling on the rails in a small, glass-enclosed motor car. One particular day, four trains had been delayed seven hours by a derailment near Seattle. Three passenger trains and a mail train all sitting in Wenatchee, waiting to go west.

Walt and his crew set out in the little rail motor car from Winton, some forty miles west of Wenatchee, to inspect a bridge over a river. This meant miles of track and a couple of short tunnels. The men figured that by the time the bridge was inspected, the first of the delayed trains would pass them on its resumed journey. They figured correctly. The plan was to take their little shuttle car off the track, let the big passenger train pass. No problem. Back on the track, they'd head through another tunnel and on to the next bridge. Again, inspection completed, they'd move out of harm's way as the second train steamed toward Seattle. This was timing a circus juggler would envy. The foreman of Walt's crew smiled in the glow of their clockwork avoiding of danger and allowed, "There's time to run down to the switch west of Leavenworth." Another siding and safety. Another inspection. The workday was ticking off nicely.

Walt balked, "Chief, that doesn't sound good to me. The train that just went by was the local, makin' all his stops. And the next train could darned well be about *ten* minutes behind him instead of twenty."

The boss assured Walt and crew they would have great visibility along the way to the next job and thank-you-very-much-but-hop-on-board-and-let's-go. So off they went. This was an electric line back in '49, and an oncoming train—like a good Quaker child—had to be *seen* ... because it couldn't be *heard*.

Well, just before the Leavenworth west switch there was a little curve, around which charged ol' Number 3 ... hell-bent for Seattle. The three startled crew members gulped with bulging eyes as the train zeroed in on their flimsy little work car. They waited to jump until the growing train was nearly on top of them—so the locomotive would smash their little car and send it somewhere behind and away from them. They waited. They sweated. They jumped.

"Boy, the last time I saw that motor car"—Walt laughed a relieved laugh—"it was clear up around the trolley wires!"

Well. Another memory of working on the railroad, frozen in drama and time. Another memory among too many memories to count. It stirred my own settled thoughts ... of trains and trips and travelers. And stations. I recalled Spokane's old Great Northern depot.

After transforming the old railroad yard into what became a World's Fair—Expo '74—grassy drumlins rise and fall around that lonely old clock tower now. But four years before the fair, when the park was just a twinkle in the Lilac City's eye, the Great Northern station was where I first breathed the beautiful Spokane air. I liked the ancient building. Its brown, weathered bricks wore the dust and soot of a century of comings and goings. The waiting room enlarged the sounds people make when they're meeting a train or waiting to board one. The aged slat-wood benches were shiny and smooth from all the sitting and rising—and sitting again—that a person does in a world governed by someone else's schedule. Benches polished by women and men anxiously awaiting a lover's return; by too many young people going off to war; by countless folks waiting a fidgety few hours for another train to take them beyond Spokane. That station and its tall clock tower stood patient and proud in spite of all the grime the traveling years threw at it. The eyes that looked out through the depot windows—with their crosshatched wires—saw somebody arriving or leaving, or they saw the conductor beckon them back to their journey. A journey that, for a few clear-air Spokane moments, threaded its way between a roiling waterfall and the stately old depot. I did like that building. And the twin bridges reaching over the river. And the way the city's lighted skyline rose from the blackened railyard.

There is a sad romance tied to every old train depot (and in the air over the spot where they were pulled down). Tom told me the Montana legend of "Old Shep" of Fort Benton. Shep was the sheep dog who went to the train station with his dying master. The man climbed on a train, but the dog was left behind on the platform. The man died in the hospital. To never return. Old Shep lived out his years under the platform at the station. The railroad people fed him, but he never allowed any to touch him or to pet him. Every day, that sheep dog met each of the six passenger trains. Hoping, I know, for his master's return. Shep is buried now on a hill overlooking the Fort Benton depot under a monument that tells his story. And wishes him peace.

We who have ridden the rails or—like Walt and Tom—have worked on them have some bright memories as we reminisce about our wanderings. And the names that pour out of this reminiscing could fill a library with adventure: Great Northern's *Empire Builder*, Northern Pacific's *North Coast Limited*, Great Northern's *Oriental Limited*, the *Western Star*, the *Mainstreeter*, the *Great Lakes Limited*, the New York Central, Penn Central, the *Super Chief*, the *City of New Orleans*, the *Black Hawk* beating the breeze from Seattle to St. Paul to Chicago. Airplanes and autos are just transportation. To me. But railroads are life: Old Shep, the Cascade Tunnel, Walt, Tom, a father and a son and a grandson, generations on their way to war, farm folk waving from an isolated house, city folk dwelling in the noise and clamor that trains author.

As the two old railroad men and I talked that rainy autumn night I thought I felt my chair lurch and sway a little in remembered rides up and down and across America. It looks like trains are slowing to a stop perhaps. And the whistle in the night doesn't tell of a train passing through the dark. It's a dirge for a life passing away.

It did somethin' to ya when you'd hear that "All aboard"
Nobody cares about the railroads anymore

Time on My Hands

I've been noticing things that need to be accomplished. My desk is cluttered. There are dirt smudges on the garage-door-opener button on the wall by the entrance to the house. (Sorry about all those prepositional phrases.) My e-mail name ought to be changed; it seemed so cute ten years ago. But now I think it's dippy and looks like something a gum-snapping sophomore would come up with ... sitting in study hall. Or detention. There's a loose floor tile in the bathroom. From when I lifted the rug beside the shower after I'd put duct tape on the bottom of the rug to keep it from slipping when I stepped out of the shower.

Stepping out of the shower, I noticed strings hanging off a couple of bath towels. My desk is cluttered. Prying the soggy tennis ball from my Corgi Wally's mouth during a round of fetch, I spotted some plaque on his incisors. The patio umbrella needs folding because I noticed it flapping in the breeze as I was channel surfing, looking for baseball or a Humphrey Bogart movie. I paused to watch a Joan Crawford trailer and was marveling at her industrial-strength eyebrows and decided I'd like a snack and heard crumbs rattling in the bottom of the toaster when I tipped it up trying to retrieve a recalcitrant English muffin wedged just below the rim of the skinny opening in the top of the toaster and I was frantic that the muffin would cool too quickly to effectively soften the peanut butter ready for a good slathering. My desk is cluttered. And if I capitalize "English," should I also capitalize "muffin"?

Uh-oh. Just this morning I detected a narrow patch of mildew on the front porch, there are a half-dozen yellowing newspapers under the bush at the top of the driveway, and we're alarmingly low on microwave popcorn.

Well, these new revelations take my mind off Wally's plaque. I need to check a dog-anatomy book to be certain dogs even *have* incisors ... or are they all just canines? Seems redundant. Somebody ought to come up with names for dogs' teeth that aren't also the name of dogs. I really ought to carry my business card in my wallet. I should get some business cards. My car needs to be washed. And vacuumed. And purged of detritus. I intend to look up the meaning of *detritus* (and exactly how to pronounce the word) so I will empty my car of the right stuff. My desk is cluttered. That green-and-maroon-sweatshirt-with-a-hole-in-the-left-elbow-and-whose-sleeves-and-neck-and-hem-are-frayed-and-Shelly-hates-it really needs some serious repair or it might just devolve into detritus.

I am listening to entirely too much sports-talk radio. Just heard a commercial for a tattoo parlor. "We're there for all your tattoo and piercing needs." Really. Needs? Who has a tattoo *need*? Who has a *piercing* need? Other than a balloon at a boring party.

I find myself worrying odd worries. In my infrequent nod to health, I took a walk today. Wally and I traveled the same route we always travel. Except in reverse. We started where we usually end and finished at the beginning. Now I'm concerned that I have added the weight and calories I usually burn when I travel in the other direction.

I am seriously thinking about making chili. Finding a recipe—somewhere; there *has* to be a recipe somewhere—and making ... chili. I am seriously thinking about doing that. I am sort of determined to make some chili. Yes. I am pretty much dedicated to the concept of chili. And tidying up my desk. And dealing with that ratty sweatshirt, de-crumbing the toaster, excising sports-talk radio from my life. Some good might come of this. I am hoping that reverse walk may have taken Wally's teeth back to a time when there was no plaque on them.

Sports and Grammar and Other Noticings

Driving along New England's charming, leafy, winding Ethan Allen Highway (Route 7) recently I passed a business called "Classic Towing." I did not know towing could reach such a height. If I ever need a tow, that's who I will call.

Just heard a report on the radio about a company that serves New York and New Jersey ... by removing gum from surfaces. Any surface. With a machine and special chemicals, gum can be removed from chair bottoms, tile floors, carpets, sidewalks, walls, metal. Anything. We had a gum-removing service in high school: Mrs. Willard, the biology teacher. She could remove gum from any student with just a cloudy glare, a piercing bark, and the threat of detention. Remember how we used to cringe at fingernails on a chalkboard? That's all in the past. Have you heard fingernails on a PowerPoint screen? I have. Nothing. Truly. No cringe. No shudder. Except at the subject of the PowerPoint. And we really *must* be careful with the fonts we choose for typing messages in this computer age. The other day I received an e-mail from a friend addressed to Shelly and me. I think the font was "Ariel 8 point." She closed with, "I love you lots." But at first glance I thought it said, "I love you idiots." Is there a support group for font-angst?

We're right in the middle of baseball's so-called post season. What an infelicitous phrase. Sounds like a high-fiber cereal. Football rumbles and rattles fall into winter with its Sunday-thudding violence, but baseball ... slow, loping, sun-splashed baseball is a saunter, a savoring of a something called "summer." Baseball is as much a season as the season in which it's played. *Post* season? That lumps it with post*modern*, post*war*, post-*apocalypse*. But the division-championship series and the league-championship series and that golden, shimmering-autumn event named—for more than a hundred years—the *World* Series are not *post* anything. They are the sum of what 162 games have added up to for eight teams in the American and National Leagues. Losers go home. Winners suit up for another day.

Oops. I have permitted a romantic bias to infect my prose. That game I recall playing and worshipping as a boy has tumbled with a clunk to this spinning earth. Steroids. Greed. Poorly executed fundamentals. Diluted talent pool (ascribed to expansion). Egregiously shoddy umpiring. And a dreadful thing that has happened to the baseball uniform. The only word that comes to my mind is ... *ick*. No longer team-color stirrups over white "sanitary hose" (how sanitary could they be?). Hat-bills uncurved. Spikes that look stolen from the Rockettes. And then there is grammar. Or its woeful absence.

The big lug athlete ought to speak the language correctly. A slugger will boast, "I hit the ball good." There are only two things with which you can hit a ball—a bat and an adverb. "Good" is neither. It's an adjective. Always has been. Always will be. If you're *trying* to hit a ball, you swing a bat. If you *succeed* in hitting a ball, you use an adverb. "Well," for example. Or "sharply" or "smartly." Baseball has rules. After you hit the ball, you don't run to third base or to the on-deck circle or out to the bullpen; you run directly to first base. And if you've hit the ball "well" enough or "sharply" enough or "smartly" enough, you continue running sequentially to second base, to third, and on to home. You cannot do such a thing *good*. You can only do it *well* or *poorly* or *not at all*. Baseball demands that you follow its rules. Language makes the same demand. The same reasonable demand. But language needs an umpire to call an offender "out!" Or Mrs. Willard to banish him to detention.

VII

Legumes and Coffee and What to Do with Bread

Gittin' Along

As I was pursuing some mundane task the other morning, the radio trotted "Home on the Range" out into the day. It was my local and loved classical music station and I didn't expect to hear *that* tune. Ever. My delight surprised me. I am not a cowboy fan. I don't like western movies. I put away childish interest in the genre way back in the distant mist of time. There was a brief period, I'll admit, when I *did* have a toy pistol and holster. A hat with a string tied under my chin. And I dimly remember a pair of boots that caused me to wonder how Gene Autry and Roy Rogers walked around in the darned things. No wonder they got into fistfights. Foot pain can make a cowpoke ornery.

And the outfits? Here were the Lone Ranger and Red Ryder galloping about the sweltering scrub plains between sun-glinting rocks and withering sagebrush ... *and they were wearing long-sleeved shirts, leather vests, floppy hats, boots, gloves, and kerchiefs cinched around their necks.* These rough, tough, rugged hombres who would spit in a bad guy's eye at the drop of a discouraging word dressed like they were about to settle into a rocking chair on a nursing-home porch. Gloves and a neck scarf? Whoa, Trigger! It had to be 98 degrees in the shade o' the cactus out there where the deer and the antelope play. And think about it: you never saw any deer or antelope playing. It was too damned hot. No wonder those ten-gallon hats were stained with sweat. Ick.

They bundled up in the blazing day but slept under the big sky in the chilled western night with just a flimsy little blanket. And their saddle for a pillow. I've only encountered two or three saddles in my time on the planet, pardner, but those two or three saddles were among the hardest and most uncomfortable accoutrements imaginable. And after spending the day lashed to the perspiring torso of poor "Ol' Paint," they had to be fragrant in a let's-hose-this-off-with-some-heavy-duty-Lysol way. More purgatory than pillow. More Dante than Zane Grey.

How about the meals? These guys claimed to be carnivores (there was always an unfortunate cow or buffalo or beefalo rotating and dripping grease over a flickering fire), but all they ever seemed to eat were ... beans. Mel Brooks celebrated that entrée in *Blazing Saddles*. Beans. Now, I love beans. Lima. Garbanzo. Baked. With brown sugar, a touch of ketchup. Maybe some little wieners cut up and tossed in. But beans are an *occasional* treat. Not an everyday meal or an every-meal day. With all else the fellas had to contend with—in that heat—why add the woe of legumes?

Perhaps snobbery is bubbling to my surface here, but each sidewinder always sported a three-day growth of stubble. Not like "Oh, I shaved day before yesterday" or "Oops, I missed this morning." I'm not opposed to facial hair—had stylishly full whiskers myself for a couple of years and loved 'em. But I think a beard ought to blossom into a beard and not look like you were too lazy to lather or just getting over the flu. Then there are the teeth. It was obvious, for most of the galoots working the cowboy shift, that the man who contracted with them to herd the little dogies from East Cupcake, Wyoming, to Lizard Lung, Arizona, offered no comprehensive dental plan. Well, blow your entire paycheck on beans ... and there're no funds left for floss.

Nope. I am not a fan of the cowboy life. Or film. I don't like it being the image other parts of the world have of this country. But I must say hearing "Home on the Range" on the radio did spur in me a mysterious need to ... well, mosey. And a strange, compelling hankerin' to rustle up some grub. Oh, I dunno. Mebbe ... *beans?*

Coffee Confessions

Too many choices in this twenty-first century. Too many. I love coffee. *Love* it. I have loved it all my life. Since I was a boy. A *little* boy. Every morning and every evening of my youth, Mom and Dad brewed coffee in a percolator on a burner on the stove. This was right around the time somebody invented the prepositional phrase (allowing me to compose the preceding sentence). Everybody used prepositional phrases back then. Even little boys. They were quite the rage.

And so was coffee. It poured into my high school years and flowed on into college. Through those years I was heated by coffee and adolescent lust. Brewed coffee. Instant coffee (I have a friend who insists that instant coffee is neither).

Coffee percolated through my radio disc jockey life in upstate New York, West Texas, and a Spokane decade in the Pacific Northwest. Coffee and the Beatles got me through those days and nights with charged vigor. Coffee brewed in the newsrooms and studios of my time in radio and television. The reporter-producer rooms of broadcasting aren't as noisy as they used to be. The computer has replaced the chunning, thumping typewriters and teletypes which sounded as soothing to me as an ocean breaking on rocks. Except when they were chattering of war. And I thought the cacophony was as eternal as that ocean. The newsroom is quieter now, but the amber odors of Columbian or Sumatran still weave through the air.

I love coffee. But now it involves choices. Too many choices. These days, when I ask for coffee, *I* am asked, "Do you want flavored coffee?" Wait a second. Do I want *flavored* coffee? Well, yes; yes, I *do*. I want coffee the flavor of ... *coffee*. I don't want cinnamon, hazelnut, chocolate, or rum. No berry. No vanilla. No caramel. No kidding. I want coffee the flavor of coffee.

It doesn't need any help. Coffee does just fine on its own. It's a perfectly strong, competent, independent, reliable, bold, warm, inviting, hearty, happy, welcome, aromatic, uplifting, upbeat, downright delighting brew ... thing unto itself. It's coffee. It's subjected—as humans are—to the daily grind, to a gurgling bath ... to arrive steaming, summoning, seducing in a mug or a cup or a carafe. Coffee needs no help. It needs no flavoring. Zucchini and shrimp and white bread need to be flavored. Desperately. They need a condiment Marshall Plan of garlic and basil and jam. But coffee needs no such assistance. It's a tough customer. *For* the tough customer. I don't want a choice. I want a cup of coffee.

But here, with a wince and a sigh, I make a confession: for the past several years I have been drinking decaffeinated coffee. At home it's easy. A cup or a pot of decaffeinated coffee. Out in the world, though—in a restaurant—I am a little self-conscious (embarrassed?) to ask for it. I feel my face warming to reflect that red-orange spout on the glass vessel containing its neutered brew. I sense a dismissive "Huh?" leveled at me. From my fellow diners and from the strangers at neighboring tables, raising neighboring eyebrows at the filling of my mug.

We truncate "decaffeinated" to "decaf." Why? To enhance communication? No. Abbreviations do not enhance communication. Abbreviations wound communication and scar language. To be cool? No. I have never been cool, and chopping up the language will not lower the temperature of my hipness. No. We say "decaf" because we are shamed. At drinking the stuff. Face it: "decaf" is coffee with training wheels. We might as well wear a beanie, hug a stuffed bunny, and hurry home before dark to drink it. "Decaf" is Nerf coffee. Little League java. Wiffle Joe. Decaffeinated is decapitated.

We who drink decaffeinated "cartoon" coffee and claim to "need our morning perk" in order to be yanked into action by the leash of day are simply saying somebody else's lines. Decaffeinated coffee cannot rev you up any more than a gallon of seltzer can launch a go-cart. Ain't a-gonna happen. But we still belly up to the bar and bark, "Hot! Black! Now!"

A Toast to Grocery Days

Toast. Nice treat. Now. And in memory. Simple. Tasty. And open to infinite enhancement. I am fond of it. In fact, I like it so much that I refer to bread as "toast sushi." It all began in my boyhood, this love of taking bread beyond baking by broiling it into something magic. From *Ann Page Bread*. Most of our food came from the tiny three-aisled grocery on the corner of Rock City Street and Main in our Little Valley. An A&P. Not the fluorescent-lighted, wide-rowed, shelf-bulging, ka-chinging, shining-cart, labyrinthine megamarket with a vast and sun-streaked parking lot that we know today.

Back in my little town, back then, people parked at an angle in the middle of Main Street. And walked in work clothes through the wood-framed door that did *not* open automatically. You had to *push* it open yourself. Nothing was automatic back there, back then. Except lots of snow from November to late March. Every Friday night my parents headed to the little A&P and I tagged along. Mom would launch into her coupon-ramble while Dad headed down the coffee aisle. Or coffee shelf, actually. He'd select a shiny red bag of Eight O'Clock Coffee beans and hand it to a guy named "Cheesy." He would pour the beans into a big chrome grinder, look at my father, and raise one eyebrow (I wished I could do that; sometimes—today as I shave—I still try). Dad cleared his throat and uttered, "Very fine." Cheesy nodded solemnly.

And as we waited, Dad would twirl his car keys and sing, "Hum diddly aye oh." The grinder ground, the keys jingled, Cheesy looked at his watch, and Dad hum-diddly-aye-ohed. Then, when it all ended, Cheesy would remove the bag, fold the wide wire tabs at the top, and hand the Eight O'Clock very fine to Dad and say, "Yup." His *yup* was like the sunset in a Hollywood western. Finished here. Time to move on.

We'd rejoin Mom as she was putting her armful of coupon-categorized groceries on the checkout counter. There were only two shopping carts in the store. One was a display of some unpronounceable ale, and the other was filled with yellowing plants. Mom was piling on the counter margarine (which my folks called "oleo"), Ann Page Bread, four cans of Real Gold Orange Juice concentrate, Raleigh nonfilter cigarettes (they came with coupons to redeem for plastic sofa covers and exotic turtles), a yellow plastic packet of dried beef, shredded coconut, an onion, a cauliflower, and a copy of the Little Valley *Hub* (our weekly newspaper, which always carried a column by Jackson Sturdley and tales of village goings-on: Nestor Kramp visiting the Bromleys while his vintage Studebaker was in the shop; a suspected break-in at Weston's Variety Store that turned out to be Nellie Weston climbing in through an unlocked window to fill a couple of sugar cones with strawberry Tastee-Freez from the shiny new just-plugged-in soft ice cream dispenser—I'd have done the same thing if I'd known the window was unlocked. The bullheaded Lucious Bleen pulled a big catch from Twombley Pond, eliciting cheers from spectators on the surrounding bank attending the Winston Skrok Memorial Hook-a-Bullhead Festival, but it turned out to be a Waring blender that had been a wedding gift in 1929 at the nuptials of Puggy Malone and Willa Dingledine. How it wound up at the bottom of Twombley Pond is still under investigation. And the high school's six-man football team was disbanded and the season forfeited because too few students turned out to try out).

As we pushed through the manually operated door and headed home, the store owner—a guy named "Guy"—motioned me over to a big barrel of candy bars—Fifth Avenue, Clark, Butterfinger, Three Musketeers, Mallo Cup, Necco—and invited me to select one. I did. And I spent the ride home from the A&P dithering over whether to open the Three Musketeers now or to wait. And dunk it in a cup of Eight O'Clock Coffee. A fine choice. Very fine.

VIII

Enticements and Mysteries

Adding Up. And Down

When I work my way through a magazine, I feel like the advertisements are speaking to me. Specifically. Directly. To ... *me*. And I wind up speaking back to them. Having a conversation. Pulling a DeNiro: "You talkin' to *me?*"

Here's a chain of hotels and resorts seducing me to book some time with them. Sapphire blue water. A smooth maroon sky dotted with puffy clouds that look more like purple meringue than meteorology. And floating above lazy volcanic hills lumped with blue-green trees. Sorry. Beyond me. I'm more of a motel guy. A cheesy painting of rain in Paris on one wall and phone numbers for pizza delivery on the other.

Then I turn the page to a photo of a necklace available at one Fifth Avenue jewelry store and a bracelet at a competing store across the avenue. I've walked between those two stores on my way to the frankfurter vendor on the corner. I think *he's* the gem in the neighborhood.

Turning over a new leaf reveals an airline eager to whisk me to a "paradise" like the hotels and resorts above. But I am a train traveler. And that track doesn't lead to paradise. Or, unfortunately, to Louisiana (another advertisement), which I *would* like to visit. Gumbo? Mmm. Jambalaya? Oh, yeah. Not only tasty, but fun to pronounce when ordering.

Hey, here's a guy in a "Roll-up Panama hat." Snazzy. He looks like he's very happy to be nearer the equator than I am. And the hat is "handwoven straw." Choice of two colors: dark natural or light natural. Natural what? Straw? What exactly is the nature of straw? Natural is not a color. It is the adjective for a noun that causes sneezing or a euphemism for "naked." Not a color. Like the mouthwash that claims on the label that its flavor is "original." I wasn't there—in the lab—that day you guys came up with the formula and flavored it. I need some specificity here. Natural? Original? Makes me think "vague …" and "sort of." The Panama hat goes for seventy-five bucks. And it's "made in Ecuador." So how can it be a *Panama* hat? Shouldn't it be an *Ecuadorian* hat? I read further to learn that I must order it from Portland. Now it has *Oregonian* connections. I can't wear a hat that's so all over the map.

Look here: an advertisement for a watch without numbers. Huh? Who buys a watch without numbers? That's like a nose without nostrils. And it's more expensive than a watch *with* numbers. How can that be? If I want a blank disk on my wrist, I can always tape a Necco wafer there. I want to know what time it is. Not to be reminded how much it cost me to *not* know what time it is.

Another airline ad offers to jet me off to Australia. Fair dinkum. I didgeri-don't think so, mate. The closest I'll ever get to Down Under is the eucalyptus oil in my Vicks VapoRub. But thanks for the thought. No, I'm thinking more in terms of an invitation I spot to vacation in Massachusetts: a full-page spread extolling the Green Monster, Emily Dickinson, and chow-dah. Oo, yeah. Fried oysters on the Cape? And a place I've never heard of: Myles Standish State Forest. Yes! I can see myself making a pilgrimage to Myles Standish State Forest. Not a woods. Not a park. Myles Standish State *Forest*. Wouldn't it be cool to be there when it goes national?

I have to stop. I'm worn out. That magazine is more work than I ever anticipated. I wonder what time it is.

Befuddlements

Oh, this old world confuses me. Really confuses me. I've always believed I was born in the wrong century. Internal combustion engines are mysteries. I know *that* a push on the accelerator will cause my automobubble to go faster, but I don't know *why*. I don't get airplanes. That whole thrust and lift thing. I don't *get* airplanes. Or *take* them. Haven't flown since I landed in San Francisco on my return from two years in Japan back in 1970. It isn't because I can't grasp the nuances of aerodynamics (I can't); it's that—at thirty thousand feet—I need more than honey-roasted peanuts to assuage my panic.

Why are Superman and Batman comic books called "comic" books? There is nothing *comic* about them. Okay, they have their lighter moments, but comedy is not their raison d'être. They ought to be *melodramatic* books. Or *adventure* books. Or *guys-in-colored-underwear* books. But not *comic* books. And why do we say something like "raison d'être" when it'd be easier to say "reason for being"? The American tongue is never sure what to do with the "T-R-E" at the end. It's not supposed to be a "truh" or a "ter." It's supposed to be said in a way for which there are no letters in the alphabet or muscles in the American throat to guide us.

Just this afternoon on the radio I heard a commercial for a fuel company urging me to buy its fuel and services by declaring, "Your family will thank you. The environment will thank you." While I have never doubted my family's comfort (or gratitude, for that matter), they have never said, "Gee, Dad, thank you for keeping the house at a cozy 68 degrees." Nor has that willow tree out on the edge of the creek ever called out with a "Way-t'-go,

91

buddy! I feel a lot greener with you at the thermostat. Oh! and thanks for not calling this creek a 'crick.' Yer the best." Did that fuel company receive a memo that says I am stupid? I am not stupid. Really. I am just confused. Born, as I was, in the wrong century.

I attend luncheons frequently. I am pro-lunch. Always have been. I ought to have spent more of my life being anti-lunch, but I support lunch. I really like it. Nice to have it sandwich up in the middle of that long stretch between breakfast and dinner, which, when I was a boy, we always called "supper." And we referred to lunch as "dinner." That was where my befuddlement began. In the movies I watched—after supper—people were always going out in the evening to dinner and I was perplexed. Forgive my digressive confusion, I was about to speak about luncheons. *Lunch* is something that emerges from a brown sack. Lunch*eon* is something that emerges from both sides of a buffet table (more confusion: that poor French T gets tossed right out of existence in the word "buffet"). There's always a guy—always a guy, never a woman—who insists on revealing how key lime pie got its name. Or how they make hot dogs. He's an expert on Lyme disease; the mud that umpires rub on baseballs before each game; Houdini's real name and where he's buried. And the fellow with all this information is often the fellow who wears suspenders while also wearing a belt. Why would he *do* that? It bemuses me.

I was befuddled by a letter from a hospital where I had undergone surgery a couple of years ago. The letter asked for a contribution. It pointed out how "a great physician can make all the difference in the world." Hyperbolic, but understandable as a hope it will lead to a monetary contribution to the hospital. Then the letter went on, "You've seen our hospital's wonderful doctors in action ..." Well, no, actually, I *didn't* see the doctors in action. I'm sure they're great. They certainly fixed me up and I will ever be grateful. But I did not see the doctors *in action*. I was under a general anesthetic. Sleeping. Oblivious. Out of it. *Never saw them in action.* Ever. They did a great job. I feel wonderful. But the only thing I can observe is a pleasant lack of discomfort, my co-pay and deductible ... and a really cool scar.

Some befuddlements are exasperations: fitted sheets ... or more to the point: *folding* fitted sheets after laundering. And those little plastic sticks stuck through the fabric of a new shirt. Straight pins in a new shirt. Stiff plastic around the collar of a new shirt. Then there is the meager dole of pork in a can of "Pork and Beans." And honking horns that claim to be car alarms. Or not having any idea what a gigabyte is. And why "byte" is spelled with a Y. If "byte" is spelled with a Y, why is "giga" spelled with an I? (Anything to do with William Blake spelling "Tyger" with a Y?) Soup and bread and pies and tuna casseroles in a restaurant being called "homemade." Beginning a sentence with "Needless to say ... ," then going on to *say* it. And by the time somebody utters, "To make a long story short ... ," it's too late. Fashion models who never smile in newspaper advertisements. Drivers in car commercials who zoom so fast and recklessly they obviously don't own the car. The guy who came up with the idea of adding some form of tomato to meat loaf. Meat loaf is just fine as meat loaf. Leave it alone. Please. This century is already enough of a mystery. Leave ... the ... meat ... loaf ... alone. Sigh. I am befuddled.

Taking the Week Off

Forgive my presumption, but if you are turning to this page because you are drawn to do so from past encounters, you will find no "A Minute with [your humble correspondent]" this week. I am taking the week and, hence, the "minute" off.[1] And *know* that *I* know my pieces take longer than a minute to read. But less than a minute to forget. I have made my "piece" with that. Sorry.

My esteemed editor moved last week's "Minute with ..." from two weeks ago (when I thought it would run in these pages) to last week (when it *did* run in these pages). I didn't understand why. There is much about this online journalism that I don't understand: labeling the photo to accompany—*illuminate*—the column is an example. It's a combination of year and month and day and writer initials and the title of the piece and then some dots (I come from a time when dots were periods. Period.) and it winds up with a little fistful of letters from the Latin alphabet.

Then there is "formatting." Time was (the same time—of periods—to which I alluded above) when "for Matt" indicated a gift or a message or a punch in the nose. Now "format" is all about spaces between one sentence's conclusion and the capital letter stationed at the start of the next sentence, guarding the jewel-like words within. My editor insists on one space. I'm from a time of *two* spaces between sentences. I still hear "Period, space, space" in my mind's ear when I come—like a stern judge—to "sentence" a thought to that space between capital letter and concluding period. I learned

---

[1] *This is from an OfficeInsight column titled "A Minute with Ira Joe."*

to do so in Mr. Lounsbury's typing class in high school and committed it to practice in college term papers and scripts for radio and television. But now I'm allotted only *one* space. I was born after World War II, but the one-space rule reminds me of stories my parents told about rationing in the '40s. Yet (and I try to feel a joy here) some concession to restoring missing spaces is made by adding a second space between paragraphs (or perhaps it's only an additional *half* space). That's nice. A kind gesture. But frankly, I'd like to have a second full space between *sentences.* It reminds me of the days when I'd type through four feet of snow on a manual typewriter seeking the warmth of hearth and home keys. If you are *my* age, you remember; you know. It is here that I sigh. Sigh.

I might have raised such issues if I were writing a "Minute with Ira Joe" this week. But I'm not. I am taking the week off, so there is no column for you to read. Nope. I am away from the keyboard and monitor. I am taking a break from rebooting, from downloading, from scrolling and surfing the web. So, there is no column this week. I hope you miss it. *I* miss it. I like the pressure of the deadline (I really do) and the challenge of rummaging away up in the word-attic, bubbling from the serendipity of rolling those things around in my mind and how they tumble on tongue and ear. I like the creak of those attic stairs and how the words blink and blush in the light of the unshaded bulb dangling from a fuzzy cord wound around a knotty beam supporting the room where words and phrases wait to be rescued and hugged and taken home.

But the words will have to stay napping in the dusty dark. We might take some future "Minute with" to ponder the paleontologist's claim that dinosaurs had tiny brains. I agree. Look at the pterodactyl. He spelled his name with a silent P. That is really stupid. Or mid-March: that touchy time of year. Should we spring for one more Chapstick before summer? Or—trying to give my life some class—how I choose to think of bread as toast sushi.

I might have juggled such notions in a column for *this* issue of *OfficeInsight,* but I didn't. I am taking the week off. There is no "A Minute with Ira Joe" today. I hope you will understand.

IX

Jog. Floss. Sit.

Sweatshirts

Okay. I know I am coming at this from a sedentary place. But I must say my say. Or type my type from that supine place. I am here to lobby for the outlawing of jogging. Jogging must be banned during the winter. Immediately. In my auto today I passed three joggers on three different streets. And it's not the first time. Just about every day I drive by a jogger or three. And the jogger worries me.

I have my hands-free telephone. I select the station on my satellite radio only when I am stopped at a traffic light or climbing into my parked car after an errand. An errand that results in M&M's peanuts on the passenger seat beside me. Sometimes my Corgi, Wally, is along, riding shotgun and on the alert for Duffy, the Saint Bernard we wave (or bark) at on a street in town. So, with phone calls and snack candy and bellicose pups vying for attention, the jogger is often difficult to see. Then there is the winter street. In New England every street is narrow. Really narrow. Has been since we were a colony and tossing tea into harbors. Narrow and potholed with a pavement undulating from the frosty games winter plays ... *and wins.*

Jogging cannot spill over to the sidewalk. The sidewalk is undulating, too. (I don't want to call the rising and falling of streets and sidewalks "heaving." Sounds too flu-related.)

But it makes more sense to ban jogging in the summer, you say? It's hot and humid and close and sticky, the air laden with a pulling-down weight. Yes. What you say is true. All of it. Ban jogging in the summer? Of course. I agree. And remember in the spring there is ragweed and pollen and waking-up-bear dander. Not good for jogging? No. The air is so chunky you have to chew it to breathe it. And you don't want to jog into a bear whose dander is up (or even just rising). Jogging has no place in the spring.

So we're down to the last season. Autumn, the "human" season, as poet Archibald MacLeish called it. There used to be the pungent sting of smoke from burning leaves. That's been outlawed. But the leaves are still raked into piles. Or blown into raging waves from lawn to lawn by hoarse and rattling leaf blowers. A jogger could trip on those dead, crackling piles. Yes! Trip and tumble and twist. An ankle. A knee. Only stories should end with a twist.

Sweatshirt. Part of the American lexicon. And folded or wadded up in every American closet. Or beside the bed. Or—in my case—draped on that exercise bike. Sweatshirt. Some name, eh? *Shirt* is shirt. Unambiguous. Comfy for either gender. Ubiquitous. Every generation has one, wears one. But *sweat*? Isn't it odd that *that* word—the verb of a body function and the noun the function produces—easily tumbles out of conversation and commerce? There are sweat socks, sweatshops, and admonitions of "Don't sweat it." I think joggers ought to sweat where they jog in winter. My advice? Give up the jogging. Give up the sweating. Set your GPS on "cheeseburger" and enjoy life.

Oral Arguments

Shelly came home from her twice-a-year dental visit with a bag full of really cool things: little chubby ballpoint-pen sized tubes of toothpaste, boxes of floss—mint, cinnamon, waxed, unwaxed, hauling-in-a-flailing-marlin-strength floss—(I love floss), little courtesy-bar-sized bottles of mouthwash, a trio of elaborately curved toothbrushes, packages of pointy picks that do the work the floss cannot (and look like something a little mountain climber would use to scale a little mountain), a refrigerator magnet with phone numbers for the poison-prevention center (for both humans and pets), and a 2009 magnetic Met schedule. Shell came home from the dentist with some of the coolest stuff I have ever seen. On my last visit I was given a box of really wimpy floss, a toothbrush with bent bristles, and a Bucky Beaver bobblehead doll. Now I understand why the cost of health care is high. The free toothpaste. Those little tubes don't contain much toothpaste. And it's been my experience that the little that is there is further reduced by a large air bubble. I am not suggesting that the toothpaste company is conspiring to short-paste the consumer, but there winds up being an even smaller amount of the "effective decay preventive dentifrice" than the container's size suggests.

As I mentioned, I love floss. And the comforting notion that it's sitting up on a shelf in the medicine cabinet just waiting for a bedtime unspooling to rid me of the detritus of my dining day. Forgive the syntax of the preceding sentence, but I am so fond of dental floss that I try to honor it with heightened language. As though G. K. Chesterton had written it. I lived for a time in Manhattan. A small but commodious apartment. It had a modest kitchen where I seldom did any cooking. I preferred to dine out. And I was always happiest in a restaurant near my apartment. I liked to be able to head home after a meal. To floss. With that as an option, I could consider more of a menu's offerings. Roast beef hash. Lumpy soup. Stringy shrimp. And offerings from the venerable chicken community: from cutlet to marsala to parmesan to fried to flame-broiled to breaded to honey-glazed to bathed in a creamy sauce that has recruited peas to come along for the ride. When you spend that much time with chicken, it always leads to the need for a serious flossing ... come the paying of the bill. I had a friend who always summoned the check by calling out to the waiter, *"L'addition, s'il vous plaît!"* Even in a truck stop. Where the wall art was posters of the Heimlich maneuver. I think he figured if he asked in French for the check, *I* ought to pay. And you know what? I agree. And I, in turn, decided that if I paid for the meal, my buddy could wait while I went home to floss.

I like dental floss so much, it—like a Beatles song—gets my mind a-wanderin'. At this point I want to consider the gift of that free toothbrush that comes from the dental checkup along with the toothpaste and dental floss. I have an *electric* toothbrush at home. The *manual* toothbrush from the dentist seems so ... so ... so 1950s. I am always expecting the dentist—wearing an "I Like Ike" button—to instruct me on taking shelter under my desk in case of nuclear attack. The toothbrush has changed since Garry Moore hosted *I've Got a Secret*, but I don't think it has markedly *improved*. It features a ribbed rubber grip down its tapered length. And it is no longer straight. It curves and zigs like a gnarled branch snapped off in a summer thunderstorm. Remember how toothbrushes used to be red? Or blue? Or sometimes orange? Now they're fuchsia or lavender or teal or vermillion. I want my oral hygiene administered by a dentist, not a decorator. Then there are the bristles. They used to be white. And level. And sitting in four orderly little rows. Now they rise and fall to varying heights within a NASA-inspired configuration. With a little pink rubber gahingus just north of the bristles that looks like a chocolate kiss. What exactly *is* that? I think I know its theoretical function. But what is it called? In dental circles, I mean. And that theoretical function is one thing. Try to *apply* it. Really. Try. To insinuate the little rubber tip between converging teeth and gums. Or gingiva (in case a dentist or tooth professional might be reading this).

That's enough to chew on for now. These thoughts are filling. Time to cap them off. A crowning finish. End of drill. Now it's time simply to rinse. But not to repeat.

Sweet Seat-ness

A new chair arrived at my door. A really cool, hip, trendy chair. I've always wished I were really cool and hip and trendy. But—*and I sigh here*—I'm not. I underwent hip replacement three years ago and the surgery has left me neither cool nor trendy. I'd wistfully hoped the procedure would result in coolness, in trendiness, but alas, it didn't. Evidence? Typing such a word as "alas." *Coolness* manifests itself in my life by how it describes ginger ale in the fridge. And *trendy*? I don't use the word *trendy*. I say, "Hubba-hubba." Kind of '50s retro-speak. The verbal equivalent of a PT Cruiser.

There are three offices in my house. Not a boast. More of a confession. The three offices are the result of slovenliness. Since Shelly's and my children have left the nest, I have filled the void with—pardon my vagueness—with ... well, stuff. And, in truth, the verb "spilled" is more apt than "filled." Since our children have grown and gone, I have replaced them with—again, ambiguity—uh, this 'n' that. My theory is that the "this-es" and the "thats" are roughly the collective weight of our moved-out offspring. Perhaps I am trying subconsciously to maintain the balance of heft between our house and the universe. I shudder that our part could tip over onto someone else's part. (As I worried forty years ago when Armstrong and Aldrin ferried those rocks back from the moon. Could the earth bear the extraterrestrial clumps without spinning in a limp off its axis and out of orbit? Sorry, but I worried.)

And not only are my so-called offices lumped with ... stuff, but there is a "pile" in one corner of our bedroom. *My* corner. It's a disgrace, I confess. Shoes. Belts. Jeans. Pajamas. Bermuda shorts. Slippers. Flip-flops. Sandals. Baseball cards. Old newspapers. Expired dog licenses. A sixth-grade report card (probably mine, because it's a faded mimeograph on which I can just barely discern the school year in Roman numerals). A coffee scoop. One green sock. A box of something from the 1960s called "Shake-A-Pudd'n." And calendars with pictures of dogs.

In one of the offices I have placed a new chair. The Allsteel Acuity. It's a sleek, sweet seat. As much going on as in the cockpit of a time-share jet: there's a "seat height adjustment" (which requires that the sitter rise when the lever is pulled). And it sports a "seat *depth* adjustment." This is *really* cool and trendy. And hip for my artificial hip. It also demands that I stand up before I "grab and hold the lever as [I] push the seat forward or backward." But it's just the seat that moves ... not the entire chair. There is a "tilt lock." Which got me to thinking about the Saint Lawrence Seaway. It offers a "locked upright work position," but also "fully supported reclining" (though my mortgage payments aren't included). It's all about choosing "the appropriate level of recline tension." I've always found that reclining *reduces* tension, and I know it's tension that drives one to recline.

Arm issues are amazingly addressed: "arm height," "arm width and depth," and "arm pivot." They can all be adjusted! Now, if only my arm could be *lengthened* I could change the light bulb above the chair so I could read a book when I am sitting in it. My All*steel* is all *black*. Except for the hubcaps on the five wheels at its base. They're chrome. With neat little blue plastic stickers that I think I will leave in place. They give the chair a kind of Smurf-burnish I like.

The owner's manual advises, "If any missing parts or loose or broken mechanisms are found," the chair ought not to be used until repaired. But if "any missing parts ... are found," it would seem to me that the problem has solved itself and the chair should go right ahead and resume its "chair-ness."

I love my Allsteel Acuity. But I already notice things are draping themselves *on* it and lumping *under* it and piling *beside* it. And I am nervous that one day I will seek the chair and it will be lost beneath things that have crept from some corner of my world which is even now filling with clutter. Like the desks I have lost count of.

Metropolis Magazine and the Vicarious Visitor

In my time with *OfficeInsight*, I have been led to look beyond its pages to the wider world of design and architecture. Here I must offer my credentials: I have none. And I am devoid of taste, I confess. I *do* have sensibility, but it's on loan and might be recalled at any time. My venturing forth (even the phrase causes my imagination to tingle) has taken me to MetropolisMag.com. There are Contractmagazine.com and Interiordesign.net, but I am drawn to MetropolisMag.com, and it's no surprise. Superman. I've been a fan of the guy in the blue pajamas ("Soop," as we insiders call him) since I was in kindergarten and eating Sugar Frosted Flakes for the free stuff that came in the boxes. So it was a cinch that I'd pick MetropolisMag.com as my stop of choice on my design-and-architecture-online-periodicals ramble. And, by the way, I come from a time when a period was a *period*, not a *dot*, and folks still inserted spaces between words just to keep things clear. But I am open to anything. Except onions in my fried rice.

I want to say that MetropolisMag.com is slick. But I can't. It lives only in my computer, not in my hands (kind of a cyber M&M's), and so, like *OfficeInsight*, it lacks the tactile charm of *The New Yorker*, *Dog Fancy*, and *Meat Loaf Monthly*. But it has its appeal. The colors are vivid and never run the risk of being out of whack in the printing (as sometimes happens in a *New York Times* sports page photo of a Met sliding across home plate with the winning run. Such an event happens so seldom that I can understand why the photograph isn't accustomed to precisely capturing it).

MetropolisMag.com trots me around the globe. I like that. Being a nonflier, the closest I'll ever get to Dubai or São Paulo, Rome or Denmark is sitting here at my glowing computer. A vicarious visitor. I stopped off at Rome's National Museum of the XXI Century Arts. It never really said I was in Rome, but that "XXI" was a good hint. Rome isn't just a once and ancient capital. It's numerals. Numerals are more than mere numbers. Numbers are in a checkbook. Numerals are on plumed helmets and Olympic Games. And Super Bowls (an American pretension). And there is the photo of a house in Denmark designed by a contemporary architect. My aforementioned sensibility shies, I'm reluctant to admit, away from "modernity." I'm a wood-paneling and flocked-wallpaper kind of fellow. I like old tube radios and chipped coffee cups and puppies who are born, not designed. So my reaction to that architect's two-story box of a Danish house is ... well, the only thing lacking is a photo on its wall of a missing child.

There is a nice metropolitan nod to New York City. Manhattan has launched an "UrbanSHED International Design Competition" to rethink, refashion, redo those ubiquitous corrugated roofs that protect pedestrians strolling the sidewalks. In the Bronx there is the new Yankee Stadium; and Citi Field now graces Queens (its predecessor, Shea Stadium, has been crumbled down to a parking lot). I like how the two stadia (remember, we mentioned Rome earlier?) have channeled the past: I am happy to note Yankee Stadium has restored the upper-deck frieze that was removed when the old stadium was "renovated" (read: historically neutered) back in the mid-'70s and that Citi Field's exterior is a poetic echo of Brooklyn's venerable Ebbets Field and it sports (great baseball verb, eh?) the Jackie Robinson Rotunda, a poignant, much-deserved honor.

The publication also addresses such issues as "Keeping Cartography Alive" (I didn't even know it was ailing) and "folding bicycles" (wow, I am still struggling with fitted sheets). Well. That's my visit to the "pages" of MetropolisMag.com. I enjoyed my time there. But I must say I am disappointed that Superman was nowhere to be found.

Now You See Him . . .

Sometimes my dog Wally is invisible. I know. Crazy. Absurd. But it's true. Sometimes he just vanishes. Briefly. He will be sitting at the top of the stairs; I see him. Next he materializes on the carpet at my feet as I sit at the keyboard typing. Or thinking about typing. Or reading. Wally is on my mind. I like his company. And I think he likes mine.

He's only two years old and always has a great prolonged romp when my children—all grown and living grown lives—visit. They love Wally as I do. And *they* are considerably more entertaining than *I* am. They get him all rowdied up. Clapping their hands. Imitating a dog's excited bark. They throw tennis balls and footballs and Frisbees and sticks and empty plastic soda bottles. Wally chases them with an exuberance that I marvel at. And envy. He treats such objects as treasures. I daydream that it would be great fun to run that fast for that long in pursuit of an old, gnarled stick. And when he latches onto the object of his mad-dash search, there is triumph in his returning trot just as there is wood in his fang-sparkling mouth. The mouth always looks like a smile, a self-pleased grin ... for chase and capture and return. His toenails click on the sidewalk like little bursts of laughter.

A moment ago he was stretching by the door to the kitchen. And now he sleeps on the floor beside me, his head heavy on my book bag. I never heard him leave his stretch and climb the five steps to a happy nap. Well, those five stairs are carpeted, yes, but I've heard them creak from treading. But Wally was one minute over by the kitchen and then, in a breathed breath, he was furry-flat on the floor. Just like that. Just ... like ... that. I never saw him coming and climbing and settling. He traveled from there to here ... unseen, undetected. *Invisible.* You don't believe it? No. *I* don't believe it. But it's true. He was over there, and now he's over here. I saw him there. I see him here. But in the *over* he dissolved from sight. In the *over* he was invisible. *How* does he do it? *Why* does he do it? Does *he* do it? Is there any *point*? Beyond a happy puzzle? A mystery whose only purpose is a head-shaking, an eye-rubbing ... a puzzled sigh at a puzzling trick or event or wrinkle? Sometimes Wally is simply, mystically, whimsically ... invisible.

Oh! He just scampered by as I typed this. Wait ... no. It was a leaf blown through the open window.

X

Dining and Stuffing and Pubbing

Restaurant Problems

"No problem," the young woman behind the counter countered when I thanked her for handing me a cup of Rhode Island clam chowder.* An odd rejoinder. And not the first time I've heard it in this young century. "No problem." The response used to be, "You're welcome" or "My pleasure." That a *problem* ever loomed in the purchase of chowder never occurred to me. But it spurred me to ponder other newly acquired restaurant problems.

Loud music. When did they start piping rock-and-roll into dining establishments? And why? Please understand that I love rock-and-roll. I've loved it ever since my brother Harlow bought the 45** of Dion and the Belmonts wailing about being "A Teenager in Love." Beatles? I worship them. Eagles? Ditto. Buddy Holly, Linda Ronstadt, Beatles, Don McLean, Beatles, Grace Slick, Mamas and the Papas, Rosemary Clooney, Dave Clark Five, Simon and Garfunkel, and Gerry and the Pacemakers. Oh! And the Beatles. Love, love, love. But at a record hop.*** Or on the car radio. On a sunny, sandy Saturday. But not in a restaurant, where I go for dining and chatting. Not rocking. Not rolling.

Once, as I waited for a friend in a favorite diner, I watched the family at a neighboring table. Mom, dad, and young son. Their food arrived—a plate of fries and a frankfurter were placed in front of the little boy. I thought, *Nice order; I might order that, too.* But the boy ignored the food and continued coloring on his place mat. And it dawned on me that I should have lived like that. In a restaurant ... well, heck, in life I have always paid too much attention to the meal. I should've done more coloring. Perhaps I wouldn't be so testy about the rock-and-roll.

* Clear broth with other chowdery things including water chestnuts.

** A vinyl record featuring two songs, one on each side. The 45 rpm disc is equipped with a hole in its center that is larger than the hole in a 33 rpm or a 78 rpm or the occasional 16 rpm record. The numbers refer to the "revolutions per minute" (that is, turns on a turntable; not to be confused with Central American uprisings). If you enjoy rock-and-roll in your restaurant, you have no recollection of 45s. Or interest in them.

*** What we called "dances" back in the days of 45s (before bands were allowed to leave cities and visit little high schools to perform music and take Brylcreem to the demotic masses).

Stuffing Thursdays

Panic. My Thursday restaurant is crowded. Again. All summer it was wide open. I'd stop by any time between eleven-thirty and one o'clock and glide right up to a vacant two-seater table. Sometimes a four-seater. Becoming a regular, I had risen above standing and attempting to appear nonchalant as I tried to catch the eye of the smiling server (who I think at one time had been a *waitress*) so she would gesture me to a seat at a table. Or a booth. Never the counter—which always has openings—because I tend to splatter in the joy of a meal. And the chairs are too high at the counter. No, I'd wait to be waited on by the waitress waltzing me to a waiting table.

And this past summer—*all* summer—I'd just slip through the door and head to a bright spot (perfect for reading and picking the onions out of the stuffing) beside the big front window festooned with tempera-paint bunnies and tulips and baby chicks. I think the artwork went up several Hallowe'ens ago and just stayed. Like a Picasso. Or a Michelangelo. Or a carved doodle on a desk in seventh grade by my best buddy, Boober.

Well, just this past Thursday I backed my 1938 Ferblungeon into a slot in the lot (I always *back* in since I saw Edward G. Robinson back his shiny roadster into a parking spot near a bank in a gangster movie). But I don't back in thinking "getaway." I back in thinking "time to dine." And I simply prefer backing *in* to backing *out*. It gives order to my Thursdays. But this past Thursday I backed in and entered the little village eatery as I always do on Thursdays. On Thursdays they serve "Fresh Roast Turkey w/stuffing, mashed potato + veggies." Says so in magic marker and bad penmanship right up there on the board hanging crooked on the wall beside a framed

115

print of bunnies and tulips and baby chicks. I think you call the place a "theme restaurant." I don't think bunnies and tulips are on the menu, but I have seen people order fried chicken.

So Thursdays I am there for the stuffing and mashed potatoes. They're exquisite. Well, the mashed potatoes are exquisite. Just enough tender lumps to make you think your mom is out in the kitchen ... distractedly mashing away. The stuffing is just a tad south of exquisite. Oh, it's bready and peppery and piled high on the plate. But ... well ... uh ... okay: the stuffing is a bit too laden with onion. *Chunks* of onion. Onion *parts*. Understand my position here. Onion—as a flavor—is fine. Okay, acceptable. But onion—as a texture—is a nails-on-the-chalkboard shudder. It's the crunch of the onion I cannot abide. If you're a vegetable and consent to peeling and to chopping and to joining a community of other foods in service to a recipe—bold, savory sausage and unselfish celery (which sacrifices its crunch for the good of the team), herbs (which don't even insist that you pronounce the first letter of their name), and spices ... if you are an edible increment as *they* are, there is no room for selfishness. "It's not about *you*, onion!" I want to yell, "It's about *stuffing* ... about blending and softening and disappearing ... leaving only your ghostly essence!" But I wind up spending part of every Thursday picking little veiny onion shrapnel out of my otherwise nearly exquisite stuffing. As the mashed potatoes sit patiently; and skin forms on my gravy.

Now summer is ended. Vacations have emptied their revelers back into town. And I have to *wait* for a table. Wait and watch plates of "Fresh Roast Turkey w/stuffing + veggies" gliding steaming and oniony by me on their way to already seated diners who haven't had to deal with crunchy onions since late last spring. Life. Wait for a table. Deal with the onions.

The Pub

There's a place I like to dine (read: eat and read). A weary old wooden structure on one end of a gravel parking lot. It's dark with rough paneling that drinks light like the happy-hour devotees down draughts at the bar.

In the dining room a woodstove, surrounded by a wrought-iron barricade, sits off against the wall. (In winter—with the stove aglow—the barricade appears *over*wrought). This room is separated from the bar by a partition and swinging doors. The whole operation unites under one simple name: The Corner Pub. It has a first name, but we townies simply use its surname: the Pub. "Want to grab a burger at the Pub?" and "I ran into Beverly last night at the Pub," or "Whaddya say we meet at the Pub, bub?"

The food is wonderful. And I mean ... won ... der ... ful. The brief, laminated menu expresses its marvels in large, bold type. And there's one whiteboard leaning against the wall and another hanging above the stove announcing specials. Scrawled with magic marker in challenging penmanship like a hasty ransom note from a reluctant kidnapper.

Shelly and I love the Pub. Now that smoking is forbidden by law and disgruntlement, conversation is more convivial ... because the air is no longer blue. We've celebrated milestones at the Pub. College degrees. New jobs. A puppy from New Hampshire.

I often drop by the Pub alone before day has been drunk by the dark walls. I listen in little earphones to music *I* choose rather than the turned-down rock-and-roll seeping from some speaker somewhere in the dark middle of the place. Maybe the paneling feels guilty about swallowing light and so it offers restrained rock in return.

Shell and I favor the table for two. And I like the table for two, too ... even when I am alone. The little table is a cozy spot with just enough room for a burger, a bowl of chowder, and a book of poems. And when the coffee comes, I always have to push aside the ketchup bottle and a fake flower to reach for a packet of sugar.

Dessert is usually declined (in case Shelly reads this). I've had far too many desserts in my spin on the planet, and the Pub's main course (never referred to as—shudder—an *entrée*) is always fine and filling. The coffee—after I dodge the ketchup and fake flower like a darting halfback—is a sweet way to bring my Pub visit to a nice-to-see-ya end.

The staff—Ila, Jeri, Aly, Steve, and Barb, the owner—are dear and intuitive. Not gratuitive. They sense my tastes on a given day. And they make it nice to be known. And welcome to return.

XI

Honestly and Carefully. Paste.

Third Grade, White Paste, and Lincoln

When I reach back in my mind for February, I rummage through myriad tucked-away images. The first to pop up is the black-and-white Motorola countenance of Alistair Cooke introducing, with Sunday calmness, the *Omnibus* episode about Abraham Lincoln. Then Royal Dano—splendid in the role of the young statesman-to-be—takes Abe from rail-splitter to debater. The drama that drooped Lincoln's eyes into perpetual sorrow could even distract me from wondering what the heck "Omnibus" meant.

The life of Lincoln did more for the month of February than we can ever measure. To me, it was a four-week festival honoring Honest Abe. I know, I know, George Washington came crying into the world on the twenty-second day of the month back in 1732. But the father of our country never stirred me as Old Abe did. I was not a fan of the tricorne hats, buckle shoes, calf-high stockings, and powdered wigs.

No, February belonged to Mr. Lincoln from the time I was six years old and discovered a little biography of the president. The book was generously scattered with black silhouette illustrations of the great man when he was a curious little boy, along with his sister, Sarah, his mother, Nancy, and his papa, Tom. I still see that book: bright orange cover and those silhouettes. Abe and Sarah helped their folks do everything. They all worked hard and yet were polite and happy all the time. Abe didn't go out with his little hatchet and chop down a cherry tree. The trees he felled were fashioned into frontier lean-tos and log cabins. They even named the logs after him. Nor did Abe go throwing money across rivers.

Ah, that sweet book and those little silhouette pictures ... *my thoughts are reaching back, reaching back ...*

"All right, boys and girls." Mrs. Remington stands cheerfully in front of the blackboard. She holds a tiny pair of scissors in her pudgy hands. "Now that we've all *carefully* traced the profile of our sixteenth president on our black construction paper, we're ready to *carefully* cut the picture out."

"Carefully" isn't an adverb Mrs. Remington tosses out casually. She always pronounces it in italics. *Carefully* is the way all third-grade teachers insist that all third graders do ... things. Walk through the hall. Drink milk. Leave the building during a fire drill. Throw a ball. Tag a girl. Cut out a silhouette of Abraham Lincoln.

The sound of careful snipping fills the air, and soon I am gazing at the undeniable likeness—in profile—of my hero, Abe Lincoln. Granted you can't really see the shaggy brows, or the teary, deep-set eyes, or the soft shadow beneath the high cheekbones. You cannot see that little wart just north and west of the thin upper and full lower lips. Or the wearily lined forehead or the protrusion of chin whiskers. Yet I have—with little snub-ended scissors—*carefully* created an unmistakable likeness of the president who gave February purpose by being born on its twelfth day in 1809.

That effort, that day inspires me to go on to render thousands of drawings of the great man. In pencil, in finger paint, watercolor, charcoal, ink, oil, acrylic, and tempera. On cardboard, Masonite, backs of envelopes, immunization records, my ankle, my brother Harlow's Boy Scout manual (bad move), and other places lost now to time. I could draw Abraham Lincoln before I could write my name.

Imagine a silhouette of Teddy Roosevelt, Woodrow Wilson, or Calvin Coolidge. Come to think of it, Calvin Coolidge looked like a silhouette even in a photograph. You and I would be hard-pressed to pick William Henry Harrison or Millard Fillmore out of a crowd of silhouettes. Or James K. Polk or Franklin Pierce. But the image of Abraham Lincoln in flat profile is a sight not to be confused with someone else. Any third grader worth his carefulness with scissors can prove it.

And why did we cut out those construction-paper images? Not merely to honor a distinguished American or demonstrate our digital dexterity. No

... each silhouette was duly scotch-taped to the windows along one wall. Perhaps they served as a sort of collective calendar for passing motorists: 34 Abraham Lincolns in the classroom windows meant only 316 shopping days 'til Christmas.

No sooner was Lincoln taped up in those windows than it was time for another third-grade rite of February: St. Valentine's Day. On which to carry to school shoeboxes filled with insipid greetings. At the A&P Mom would pick up a plastic bag of "Fun Valentine Sheets." And I'd spend the evening of February 13 tearing along the dotted lines. *Carefully.*

The message each valentine sports is dippy, even to the unblossomed perception of an eight-year-old:

Roses are red.
  Onions are smelly.
  Be my valentine
  Or I'll sock you in the belly.

or

How do I love thee?
  Let me count the ways.
  On second thought,
  Forget it.

or

Violets are purple
  Arithmetic is dumb.
  I like you better
  Than Dubble Bubble bubble gum.

or

I used to think
  My dog was neat.
  Then I met you.
  Now I think he's neater.

I pick out the "best" of the lot—a pretty tough task; the lot is none too good—and address them to my beloved girlfriends. Then I hurriedly relegate the remaining cards to the rest of my classmates.

On the morning of the big day—third grade is crammed with *big* days—I lug my boxful of valentines onto the bus. At school I step down from the bus, move through the February cold (with its subtly blended odors of bus exhaust, chimney smoke, and last night's Vicks VapoRub), and slip into the wiggly heat of the school building. The morning unfolds in encounters with addition, subtraction, the major exports of Argentina, Aunt Em's letter in *My Weekly Reader*, and an interrogation about my alleged role in a burnt-sienna-crayon-having-been-ground-into-the-auditorium-carpet incident.

But finally, party time. We carry our chairs into a semicircle (all through my grade school years I wished for enough additional classmates to, at least once, form an *entire* circle).

And valentines find their ways to their intended; and a heart-shaped, semicircle time is had by all. The girls band together and present Mrs. Remington with a special valentine and a box of Fanny Farmer chocolates. And as she reads—with moistening eyes—the frilly, lacy card, we boys—in subdued unison—feign terminal nausea.

I've heard of children being too excited to eat (one of life's experiences that I have avoided), but some fellow third graders seem so moved. A few mothers would send a batch of iced sugar cookies to us revelers. Too excited to eat? An iced sugar cookie? Yeah, right. I down enough to give my complexion a greenish cast. That stamps the party—for me, at least—a bubbling success.

So, with our Lincoln likenesses fading in the late-winter windows and valentines curling in shoeboxes, we've spent exactly half of the February allotted to us. Only *one* big day remaining. Washington's birthday. An anticlimax. To me. Oh, I'll trace a black construction-paper silhouette of a fellow with a ponytail and cut it out, but not very carefully. (Mom and Dad took Larry, Harlow, and me to Mount Vernon one summer. But the visit wasn't stirring. How anyone could live in a house bigger than a school gym and tidier than a hospital puzzled me. I also wondered how George and Martha moved from room to room. Each doorway had a little velvet rope hung across it.)

I will patriotically conjure up those images when Mrs. Remington directs our thoughts to President Washington. An honest man, good surveyor, courageous general, self-deprecating president. I know all that. But it is no use. My mind swirls with log cabins and a speech at Gettysburg, books read by the fireplace, and a proclamation declaring all people are, indeed, equal ... and free. I suspect that Gilbert Stuart abandoned his portrait of Washington for one of the very reasons *I* couldn't work up enthusiasm for him—wooden teeth.

February is the littlest month, as months go. But a great little month. It even gets an extra day every four years. You don't give extra days to crummy months. And now February is solemnly designated "Black History Month." I'm sure Mister Lincoln would be moved and proud.

Everything changes when we grow up. A Lincoln is a something wealthy people drive. And Washington (the DC one) is where many of the Lincolns are driven. Valentines are television actresses or baseball players. And St. Valentine's Days stir gloomy rememberings of a massacre in Chicago. Ah, me ... what we could accomplish with scissors, construction paper ... and being careful.

XII

Springing, the Bard, and a Jar

A Fling Flung

Thumbing through an office-furniture magazine, I was drawn to the photographs accompanying the article about the "Global Spring Fling" in Manhattan which happened, actually, in the departing days of winter. But spring is more a thought and a wish before it blossoms into a season. The thinking and the wishing begin when the sparkle of the December holidays settles like a sunny dust to the pine-needled carpet. (And, in truth, it was an online magazine I was viewing, and I *know* one does not *thumb through* on online magazine. One thumbs through the Sears catalog and one's always-have-intended-to-read-but-haven't-yet-done-so copy of *Pride and Prejudice*. Because no species of mouse—four-legged or computer-aged—has or responds to thumbs, one resorts to "scrolling" or "clicking" or verbs that are spelled with only "1s" and "0s" and cannot be pronounced).

And the attending fling-*ees* are smiling at the fling-*ing*. They seem genuinely happy with the proceedings. *I* smiled at an action shot of snack plates carried by uniformed servers. I cannot tell from the photo, but I'm betting there were plates of little skewered chunks of chicken. Or water chestnuts wrapped in bacon. Or scallops wrapped in bacon. Ever notice that life brightens, that doubts dissolve, that phobias fade when you wrap them in bacon? I'd have thought Julie Andrews would have included bacon among her favorite things when she sang to the von Trapp children, wouldn't you? Then again, perhaps the servers were offering egg rolls or mini spinach quiches or wavingly pierced pieces of rare roast beef (which I'd have declined because I like my roast beef as I like my sushi: well done). I do wish the photo had focused more closely on the plates. Were there celery chunks with cheese in their green troughs? Or bruschetta brushed with garlic and littered with tomato shrapnel? Crackers? The miraculous cracker is a fine fling's feature. The cracker will support any topping: creamy, meaty, veggie. Could the servers be serving cheese puffs? I love cheese puffs. Pretty much any kind of cheese. Especially when it's puffed. Sometimes I am so eager for a cheese puff that I clumsily grab one (or three) from the plate and pop them right into my mouth ... without daintily accepting the napkin from the patient, smiling server dressed in black and white. And—cheeks puffed with puffs—I blush and mumble a cheese-puff-muffled thank-you.

I see from the account of the occasion that there *were* pigs-in-a-blanket. Nice touch. Good choice. And a great space filler between the grilled shrimp and the stuffed mushrooms. I am always awed by stuffed mushrooms. The care they require, the meticulousness. Like building a boat in a bottle. Like darning socks on a speeding train. Okay, I've never done that. Or needed to. But I suspect they're much like stuffing mushrooms. And worthy of admiration.

The event has come and is ended. The fling is flung as spring is sprung. As the Ming dynasty is Mung. And a dead king is a kung. Or when the song is sung, "Zung went the strungs of my heart." It's how "ging-ho" culminates in "gung-ho" and table tennis bounces from ping to pong to pung. May all our flings be famously flung. And wrapped in bacon.

Curbing

Ah, garbage day. Motoring along my street on this day is like riffling through a collection of short stories. A tale at the end of every driveway. Gee, my neighbor drinks that brand of beer? And quite a lot of it. Wow. Those folks bought a trampoline? They never struck me as trampoline types. Another video game for the house with all the children? How many does that make now? Games and children? Sure wish I were better acquainted with that young couple on the corner, because every garbage day there are a bunch of empty macaroni-and-cheese boxes in their little blue bucket. Melted cheddar and elbow pasta can sure take a fella's mind off the secrets *his* trash might reveal.

Now, hold on: *the shoe trees were a gift.* I tried to hide the box they came in at the bottom of the bundle. I'll never use them, but they *were* a gift. I can't regift them, because I took the box they came in out to the curb. And the economy pack of vitamins-for-people-over-sixty was just too good of a deal to ignore from the store the size of a B-52 hangar where they sell cinnamon buns and snow tires and factory-flawed blue jeans and plastic platters of shrimp. Right next to each other. And the case of beer *I* brought home is non-alcohol beer. Maybe I ought to go up to the end of the driveway and write "non-alcohol" with a magic marker in large letters on the emptied box. You know ... just in case. Oh! And the big plastic bag that the circulatory-supporting athletic knee socks came in can always be explained as belonging to an older relative who spent the night after missing his flight. Of course, it's no one's business; but you know ... Wait a minute. *My* garbage is *my* garbage, I mean come on.

131

It's not like I ordered another muffler for the vintage Studebaker as my collector neighbor did on the next block. That gas guzzler really goes through the parts: mufflers, carburetors, hubcaps, steering wheel knobs, side window wings, Styrofoam antenna balls, chrome hood caps, synthetic mirror-frame fur, vinyl driving gloves with the ends of the fingers nipped off, global-positioning systems (wonder if they only show roads winding through the 1950s ...), and stuff like that. As if anybody would want such things. Or notice. Certainly not I.

Or the middle-aged couple in the clapboard ranch seven doors down. Another treadmill? They really go through the workout equipment. And sweat suits. I see gym-clothing bags all the time at their curb on garbage day. The two of them don't seem to be in particularly great shape, either. Not that I've ever put a treadmill box or sweat-suit sack out at the end of the driveway on garbage day, myself. I'm just saying ...

And with environmental concerns finally coming to sit in the fronts of our minds, the curbside stories grow richer ... in color and detail. There is the large (usually) brown or (sometimes) green (plastic) receptacle rather than the former (galvanized) can. My receptacle has a guiding arrow on the cover instructing me how to aim the can at the street. That old, arrowless, round, dented garbage can of yore used to lean—rusty and fetid—waiting for the dog to bark at the whiskered, cigar-chomping guy in dusty coveralls to lumber down the screech of his brakes and clunk the morning with a metal-on-metal meddling in sound. No more garbage *can*. Now we have the garbage *container*. We have the recyclable *container*. And on one morning each week, they usher out of our lives and minds the stuff we've trashed. Garbage day. Huh. Just another number on the calendar.

B and B and B

A getaway weekend. To a New England bed and breakfast. I love the clarity of *bed and breakfast*. Some people truncate it to *B and B*. Not I. I am anti-abbreviation. Ultimately, abbreviating things doesn't shorten communication. It lengthens it. Quick: what does *MO* represent? Missouri? Montana? The chief Stooge? Right. *You* don't know. *I* don't know. And so *MO* becomes an obfuscation, not an abbreviation. And the guy who invented it is a meathead deserving a poke in the eye.

But I digress. Sorry. The inn Shelly and I check into is lovely. Yellow clapboard. Gleaming green shutters and frames. I think the architectural style is Federalist. I'm not certain, but I *think* that's the style. Yes, Federalist. I know it's not Lego. It has to be Federalist.

The check-in station is a snug little alcove with room for only a slim attendant. There is a wall-mounted rack of wooden shelves for mail and messages. Above that is a digital liquid-crystal clock/thermometer (with indoor and outdoor readings: indoor? 68 degrees. Outdoor? 47. 3:14 p.m. in both locations).

A tall, smiling lady records our credit card on the inn's colonial computer, then shows us to our room. On the second floor. Up a narrow flight of carpeted stairs with a substantial wooden banister ... all shiny and smooth, it begs for a good sliding-down. But, sigh, I am too old to slide down a banister. And clearly nearly too old to climb the stairs lugging a suitcase, a garment bag, and a canvas sack stuffed with books, sweatshirts, water bottles, and a can of cashews while Shelly chirpingly chats—empty-handed—with the tall, smiling lady—also empty-handed—who is escorting us to our room.

Elevators? Who needs 'em? (*I do ...*)

Our room (number 15) is a brightly windowed corner with sunlight pouring through white curtains over white windowsills under a white ceiling. I feel like a drafted aspirin as I squint through the sweat seeping from my eyebrows. Prompted, maybe, by my bellhop-less luggage lug up the stairs. My muscles groan as I drop the burden on the bed. As she hands me the room key, the tall, smiling lady asks if she can help with anything else. I exhale a "No, thanks," and hope I don't splatter her with my streaming perspiration. She leaves and Shell remarks how pretty the wallpaper is. I have trouble focusing on the pansies and lilacs as rivulets cascade over my eyes.

The king-sized bed is immense. A King-George-the-Third-sized bed. Biggest bed I've ever seen. And overkill for the room it occupies. I have to inch sideways to reach the bathroom. Really big bed. Deserves its own zip code. I am talking big bed here.

The bathroom is not as big as the bed (that bed—did I mention?—is huge), but large and—forgive me—commodious. The tub rises high and demands the agility of a gymnast to gain access. Not constructed with a hip replacement or torn quadriceps or arthroscopic knee surgery in mind. But it's a tub that has led to a few of those. The tub and that damned staircase. Yep. Relaxing weekend.

At least when I scale over the bathtub wall and slide into its porcelain depths, there'll be a steaming shower to coax my taxed tendons back to pre-B-and-B comfort. Well. Let me tell you. When I go to shower, I discover the fixture is not mounted on the wall. It's a detached nozzle at the end of a forty-foot hose. Are you with me? The water spews from that nozzle, that hose ... requiring me to hold it in one hand while trying to perform my ablutions with the only other hand I have. Turns out I am a two-handed showerer. Never thought about it until I stood all sudsy and unfulfilled by the whole awkward arrangement. I cherish my shower. So much so that I always applaud when I finish. But I cannot applaud when one hand is holding the loofah and the other is holding the nozzle. This was a disaster. A *half* shower. Hygiene without the *high*.

After scaling the wall to escape tub and turmoil, I discover that I have forgotten to pack my blow-dryer. Panic. No blow-dryer? After a one-handed *non*-shower? A comb-over tragedy. But miracle of miracles, Shelly hears my cry as my soapy feet slap down onto the old, cold tiles. She senses my anguish and slides down the banister to ask if there is a blow-dryer anywhere in the inn. Yes. Gloriously, yes! It seems this is not just a B and B. It's a B, B, and B. Bed, breakfast, and blow-dryer.

She returns triumphant. And what a blow-dryer! It rivals the king-sized bed and length of the shower hose. It sports a power cord long enough to permit me to dry my hair in the parking lot if I wish. I stand before the bathroom mirror with dryer in one hand and styling brush in the other and wait for the electricity to travel from the wall outlet to the barrel. The day is saved. I look darned spiffy and emerge from the steam ready to try to talk Shelly out of visiting every antique shop in western Connecticut. I lose. But state my case so fervently ... that I need another shower. Yep. A relaxing weekend getaway ... got away.

Safety First: It Could Be Verse

We must not allow April to pack its bags and return to wherever it spends the other eleven months without noting its venerable place in the calendar. April is National Poetry Month. Because it was in April that Shakespeare was born. On the 23rd. Back in 1564. Back in Stratford, England. So it's fitting to honor poems by honoring the gentleman who lifted our lumpy mongrel language into exquisite verse.

April is also Work-Zone Safety Month. A sign noted the designation as I motored my automobubble into a re-paving area on a lovely, poetic interstate highway in New England. It's wonderful to underline the need for safety in our over-55-mile-per-hour age. But why devote just one month to it? Does that mean May through March is floor-it-and-forget-it time? Are those intrepid folks in scuffed work boots expected to doff the orange vests and yellow hard hats when April ends? And the motorist can return to zooming like a solipsistic jerk?

All through the year we are reminded that "Fines are doubled" for crimes committed in a highway work zone. Good idea. (Doubling the fines, I mean; not committing the crimes.) The work-zone worker ought to be able to arrive at the job and depart and spend all of the time there in ... well, *safety*. Even when it looks more like a stand-around-and-lean-on-the-idle-bulldozer zone. The point of the place (vis-à-vis safety) is the people. Not the activity (or lack of it). And our collective and individual regard for their safety ought to be eternal. Or at least year-round.

The same applies to National Poetry Month. It ought not to be confined to a single month, like an inspired muse in a bad limerick. We've surely heard

T. S. Eliot's claim that "April is the cruelest month," but that disregards the kindness April exhibited by giving us William Shakespeare. Eliot is clearly in a snit (the comment opens his grumpy-bear "Wasteland"), and he continues: "breeding / Lilacs out of the dead land, mixing / Memory and desire, stirring / Dull roots with spring rain." Calm down, crabcakes. *It's National Poetry Month.* Be happy. Get your word's worth by wandering "lonely as a cloud" and serendipitously encountering "a crowd, / A host, of golden daffodils." A fellow named William Wordsworth was on a walk in England's Lake District with his sister, Dorothy, when they experienced that flowery hour. I don't know if they were hiking through April, but they could have been, they *should* have been. A poem bubbled up and out of that hike. And how fast could they have been moving? Not very. No danger to any road workers in the neighborhood.

I've even taken a shot at musing the month in my poem "An April Day":

In the sun
   a wind bothers
   the boughs
   of a pine
   across the street.
   It ripples
   a canvas awning
   as if thumbing
   the pages
   of an old book
   so loved,
   so read,
   it sits open
   and holy
   like a bible
   on the table.

There's no rent

in the sky,
no broken blue,
to tell
where the wind
slipped from.
It clears spring
for the sun
and the budding
to come.

Now, I am admittedly a minor poet. But I prefer to regard "minor" not as *obscure*, but as under twenty-one years old. It's nice to be young again. As Wordsworth exults, "then my heart with pleasure fills, / And dances with the daffodils."

Not only was Shakespeare *born* in April—on the 23rd—he *died* in April—on the 23rd. A sobering symmetry. But Shakespeare's point is that he lived, not that he died. We all die. He just happened—while he was here—to put the words that belong to all of us into a most moving and memorable order. Ever. Thank heaven for April. Thank heaven for a poem. And a road beneath our wheels.

Jarring the World

The mayonnaise container. I didn't think it could do anything more remarkable than contain mayonnaise. Then along came my sojourn in Mrs. Currie's fifth grade. And May warming by the nearness of June. The leaves were finally and fully formed, unwrinkled, undrooping, and giving shade to the grass and ground. Like Thoreau, it was time to go into the woods.

Mrs. Currie had a weekend cabin on a little pond at the end of an endless dirt road five miles from the center of our village. Other cabins ringed the pond, and to go there in the heat of summer was special, enchanting. Jumping from the dock into the water made for a cooling that still splashes in my memory. Mrs. Currie's gift to us ten-year-old scholars as the academic year neared its finish was a picnic at her little cabin.

The modest resort was called "The Rod-and-Gun Club." And one had to be a member or an invited guest. I never saw a rod or a gun. A few rowboats, Adirondack chairs painted calm red, dogs running or sleeping (nothing in between). And inner tubes. They were a great fun of summer. Black rubber with the protruding air nozzle that scraped the sides of a generation of giddy swimmers. You don't see inner tubes anymore. They're gone. The way of army surplus pup-tents and Clark Bars and Deputy Dawg cartoons. And I miss them. Now that the scars on my ribs have healed.

And I miss the huge cafeteria-sized mayonnaise jar. There were twenty-three jars on yellow bus number five that lumbered from Little Valley School to Mrs. Currie's Rod-and-Gun cabin that May day way back when every rock-and-roller who ever lived was *still* living. Twenty-three mayonnaise jars for twenty-three fifth graders on an outing. The jars rattled and we fifth graders fidgeted as the bus dusted along the dirt road. The girls giggled and blinked in the sunlight flickering through the leaves and windows. We boys exulted in loud voices—trying to make them deeper—about the deer and panthers we knew to be prowling the woods.

As we disembussed, each of us was handed a mayonnaise jar. Glittering. Clear. And nearly the size of the fifth grader who cradled it. We bounded into the flower-flecked garden of Mrs. Currie's cabin. To feast on hot dogs and Queen-O orange soda and rhubarb sauce. Marshmallows and pretzels and chips. The girls fed the visiting dogs. We boys fed us boys. To this day, I love a burned and blackened hot dog as much as I love rain thrumming on the roof or checking a baseball card to see how many homers Yogi Berra popped in 1957 (twenty-four). There was no swimming that day. The pond shuddered at the thought of twenty-three fifth graders roiling its roily waters ... and we'd have had to wait the obligatory hour after downing the frankfurters, chips, and Queen-O for it to be safe to swim. No, this was a visit to the woods, not the shore. So we stayed dry. And high, nevertheless, in the joy of sunlight and pickle relish. And though it wasn't a swim, magic still came after lunch: *the expedition*. To transform our mayonnaise jars into terrariums. Or terraria, if you're reading this in ancient Rome.

Mrs. Currie led us into the woods and guided us with our little plastic scoops to fill the bottom half of the mayonnaise jar with the black, loamy earth sponging beneath our feet, beneath the trees. Into that dirt we poked the roots of a variety of growing treasures: false indigo and blue false indigo to wild blue lupine to common lupine (mine was a most egalitarian terrarium), purple giant hyssop (causing me to consider the fifty-first Psalm), slender vetch and cow vetch (we were in dairy country, after all), common skullcap, smaller skullcap, and the ominous mad-dog skullcap; there were blue toad*flax* and ghostly toad*stool* (which always seemed something of interest to a toad's physician), forget-me-nots and a couple of gentians, a here-and-there astor ... from bushy to showy to bog. It was a botanical banquet.

I also found a tiny tree frog, named him "Carl," and placed him gently on the floor of this verdant neighborhood-in-a-jar. With the dirt and plants and Carl ensconced, I covered the jar's mouth—as urged by Mrs. Currie—with Saran Wrap secured by rubber bands. The plastic wrap was the key. Photosynthesis kicked in. Sunlight and the jar's inherent moisture cycled around that little environment as it does in the wider world. Through the slow summer, evaporation from the plants and loam would culminate in condensation on the underside of the Saran Wrap. Drops formed and joined and enlarged. Then gravity would prompt the water to fall—to *rain*—back down on the square foot of real estate below, bathing plants and dirt and Carl. "Wow," I thought back then. "Wow," I still think today.

Every day I pondered the sweet scene. The plants. The rain. Carl. As summer began in earnest, Carl seemed to grow listless. When I noticed him fashioning a rope and noose from the tendrils of a miniature fern, I opened the Saran Wrap lid and lifted my tree frog to freedom. He was never really mine. He was never really "Carl." He was a tree frog. And belonged in the woods. In the trees. "Wow," I thought back then. "Wow," I still think today.

XIII

Tempus Fugit

Hundreds of Years

Tri- and bi-. Sounds like a rent-to-purchase franchise. Or a late-night cable show. It's neither. It's centennials. A *tricentennial*. And a *bicentennial*. I am in the middle of both. How could two auspicious celebrations converge in my experience, in my spin on the planet? I can't say.

The county where I was born and raised is in western New York. Cattaraugus County. It's celebrating its two hundredth anniversary. "Cattaraugus" is a native American word. I have no idea what it means. I should. I've had two hundred years to find out. It was in the midst and lore of the American Indian that I grew up. Imagining the presences and the ghosts that "Cattaraugus" conjures.

And now my county is two centuries old. A dotted line was drawn through the leafy woods, up and down the humpty hills and across lazy lakes and juddering creeks. Or "cricks" as we are wont to call them in Cattaraugus County. A lovely land that was a grand place for coming of age. I was your typical dusty boy running through the clover and hay, aiming my Schwinn in the summer air, scuffing my sneakers over the fallen fall leaves and clinking my "arctics" along the snow-plugged sidewalks. "Arctics" were black rubber boots. With four metal buckles to secure their accordion fronts. Those buckles metal tinked and clinked in the numbing cold. I think that was the only place such boots were called "arctics." They fit over one's shoes. And they looked really dorky, but they kept my feet reasonably warm as I rode my sled ("going sliding," as we called it) or shoveled the driveway ("*^!#!!!," as we described it) or peddled papers ("peddling papers," as we explained it).

My town is the county seat. Little Valley. The center of the county government. Our weekly newspaper was *The Hub*. So named because Little Valley is situated in the geographic center of Cattaraugus County. The paper's gone and I miss it. It's still the best name for a newspaper I've ever encountered. *The Hub*. I worked for that paper when the county was only 156 years old. I never imagined the paper wouldn't make it to the bicentennial.

I'd been invited back to ride in the celebratory parade this weekend. In a convertible. That's frightfully optimistic for western New York in late September. A convertible? I recall snow falling on many a September day. And a white Hallowe'en was not unheard-of.

The other centennial that has yeared its graying head is the *tricentennial* of the town where I now live: Ridgefield, Connecticut. For the first hundred years of these United States, the nation pretty much hugged the Atlantic Seaboard. We ventured west as a migrating people slowly. That's why western Connecticut has a one-hundred-year lead on western New York. Life here is different than life there. We're a Revolutionary War–era town. The locals battled the British back in April of 1777. Then the town was already sixty-nine years old. And not amused by taxation without representation. Benedict Arnold fought in the fight. He was still on the home team and hadn't jumped to "them" as a free agent. There's an old tavern in our town with a redcoat cannonball lodged in its facade. I drive down *Barrack* Hill every day. It's where the British encamped. Ever notice how soldiers *encamp*? And guys in T-shirts and flannel merely *camp*? (Being a loyal Democrat, I think of the road as "Barack" Hill.)

A *bi*centennial. A *tri*centennial. That's five hundred years' worth of centennialing, bub. Five ... hundred ... years. Whew. I need a nap.

Tearing Along the Southern Tier

Last weekend's hundreds of years involved hundreds of miles. Shelly and I motored from Connecticut across New York State. For Cattaraugus County's bicentennial parade. A 350-mile trip. Along Route 17 with its red-white-and-blue signs portending a change of name to "Interstate 86." The road also bears a poetic nickname ... the "Southern Tier Expressway." I like *that* name. And I like it that the sign carries a stylized depiction of a Native American painted in bold green.

Shelly was reading and I was thinking as we bumped along the pavement. Winter isn't kind to northeastern America's roads. And Route-17-soon-to-be-Interstate-86-the-Southern-Tier-Expressway suffers from frost heaves and plow scars and the flapping tires of trucks and cars and motorcycles. I wondered if the transformation from 17 to 86 would be an *up*grade of the *road* grade. Will the snow-snakey curves undergo a gentle straightening? Might the shoulders widen and smooth? The traffic-lighted intersections will surely disappear into humming overpasses and underpasses ... won't they?

The countryside needs no fixing. It's stunning. A hilly, tree-colored undulation from Pennsylvania to just south of Lakes Ontario and Erie. Autumn was already dabbing late September with yellow and gold, russet and red. Just west of Roscoe (the town, not your uncle from Eddyville), the sky filled with Canada geese. *Filled*. I couldn't count them and keep my hands at 10 o'clock and 2 o'clock on the steering wheel, but it was a profusion of silhouetted geese on their way to that place where geese spend winter. A happy-sad sight. A flying bird always makes me happy. But they're taking

147

with them a last little scrap of summer ... fading, folding, flying away on the wings of geese. Sad.

As we zoomed on, it occurred to me that we ought to name our *roads* as we name our *towns*. Enough with numbering them. Let's give Route 17 a parting gift of officially calling it "the Southern Tier Expressway." And put Interstate 86 back in the box. We crossed exits (also always numbered, not named) for "County Road 28" and "State Route 11." Perfectly lovely lanes to the eye, but they make a map look like Mrs. Willard's ninth-grade algebra homework. I don't want to travel a road that I might flunk.

The sweetly named Susquehanna River plays curve and split along the route, as if it's reluctant to flow into Pennsylvania and on to the south. There's the Allegheny threading between Olean and Salamanca before it decides to slip south to Pittsburgh. And the creeks aren't numbered, either. They are charmingly *named*. Cayuta, Silver, Red House. They're poems to experience, not equations to solve.

The U-turns are ubiquitous. And designated as 3212-K and 60622-Y. Can you imagine the bureaucratic nightmare it is to conceive the numbers and relegate them to a map or a grid or a wherever-they're-relegated? And U-turns are not even ours to use! They're there for the police and snowplows. Can't we at least name them "Oliver" or "Yogi" or "Blanche"? I mean the U-turns, not the police and the snowplows.

Then, as I neared my home village—Little Valley, the county seat of Cattaraugus County—there was a multitude of little birds (sparrows? starlings? robins? wrens?) clinging to a sagging wire between weathered telephone poles leaning over lolling Holsteins and Guernseys in a pasture by a barn. The sky was gray but bright enough with day and autumn to blacken the birds against it. Their features were gone. Only their shapes remained. My grandmother once told me that birds congregating on a telephone wire predict rain. And soon ... it poured.

To celebrate Cattaraugus County's two hundredth birthday, we paraded and waved; we smiled and chatted. And I was happy, in my old home ... from a drive through the loveliness that is autumn along a highway that sits in my heart as a name and a sweet memory. Not a number.

XIV

Blossom Browsing

Et Tu, Arbutus?

Nobody was smiling. None of the customers. At the nursery. I seldom visit a nursery. I love flowers. I adore flowers. The colors. The smells. Little water globules on fuzzy leaves. How they enliven any green they grace. I love flowers. I'm not unique. *Everybody* loves flowers. And many people visit nurseries. To bring flowers home for planting in pots and window boxes and old weathered barrels by the sidewalk. Many people do that. My Shelly does that. But I don't. I love flowers. But I don't *do* anything with that love. So I seldom visit a nursery. But today I did.

We were on another errand—Shell and I—when she said she'd been looking for a particular plant for a particular spot at our house and asked if I'd mind stopping at a nursery. We've stopped at nurseries a few times in our romance. Shell goes into the plant plant and I sit in our 1938 Ferblungeon, roll down the window ... and read. I always keep some Mary Oliver in the car. Or Hemingway. Or Frost. You have to be careful with Frost, especially *late* Frost. Around plants.

Today I didn't have a book. I don't know why not. Just walked bookless out of the house and arrived at the nursery with nothing to read. So I decided to go in with Shelly to browse. That's a sort of library verb. *Browse*. Oh, you can browse in a hardware store or a clothing store. You can browse the Internet. But *browse* doesn't sound like a nursery verb. I don't know a better verb, so *browse* must suffice. Into the nursery we went. Why is it called a "nursery"? There are no nurses. Nor babies. It's pretty much a blooming, blossoming, budding business. With hangey-down hoses and puddles on the cement floor and an all-day dew on the windows that curve from earth

151

to sky and back. A sort of metaphor for life. It ought to be called a *bloomery*.

The folks at the nursery were a friendly lot. They *were* smiling. In the aisles. Beside the profuse pansies and nasturtiums (nasturtia?) and trailing arbutus (trailing arbuti?). Even the guy steering bags of mulch from point A to point Bee (pollen headquarters) ... smiled. The nursery folks smiled as they answered questions about fertilizer (you have to admire anyone who smiles when speaking of fertilizer). I heard the word "manure" and looked at the two people from whose chat the word emerged. The nursery person was smiling. Now, that's a gift: manure ... and a smile. The customer was serious. *Very* serious. Apparently the customer—a gray-haired lady in a sweatshirt with sequins on the right sleeve and sweatpants with sequins on the right pant leg and sneakers that complemented the rest of her sweat attire. Even her sneakers had sequins. Just a few. I'm not talking sequin blizzard here. No. Just a nice scattering of sequins that made the fashion statement, "Yes, I am in sweat clothes, but I don't plan to sweat. I have sequins."

There were other customers. A guy with a mustache and black socks and ... *sneakers*. Another woman in jeans and an airy blouse and an airy scarf draped about her neck. It was pretty warm and muggy, not really scarf weather, but I seldom go to a nursery, so what do I know? Her sneakers were mostly white, but with a dash of pink in the laces and on one side. None of the customers was smiling. In fact, they were all frowning. Serious, furrowed-brow, narrow-eyed ... frowning. I looked at Shelly a couple of aisles away. She was rubbing a leaf with finger and thumb, concentrating ... and frowning. In a brief, cloudy moment behind a window I caught my reflection. *I* was frowning. So it couldn't have been sneakers too tight or sequins too bright. I was wearing sandals. Without socks.

I understand the nursery folks being happy and bubbling. The bud business looks better than blooming, it seems to be booming. I'd think plants would make us shoppers smile. At a pet store people are always smiling. You can't frown when you hang around a puppy or a turtle. Hardware? Music store? Toy store? Smiling, smiling, smiling. No frowns at the ice cream shop. Or even at the shoppe. So why the frowns at the nursery? Could it be we were all feeling impatiens?

XV

Baseball and Mortality

Base Hits and Obits

They've finally moved the obituary. My newspaper of choice is not just a newspaper. It's an event. An everyday rite to which I look forward. And there is an order to my fulfilling the rite. First ... front page. Seeing the ink confirms that *I'm* still here ... though the world and hope for peace remain sorry and sinking. Then I turn to page two of the front section to locate the obituaries. Forgive me, but I do. I've spoken with others who say they also go early in their papers to the obituaries. Death is not only inevitable; it's interesting. Sad. Tragic. Untimely. But compelling reading. And lately the morning mourning is presented in that front section where the news and views bubble and fizz.

After scanning the death notices, I turn to the Sports section. My athletic days were few and unexceptional ... in both success *and* failure. I never hit a homer or scored a touchdown. Because I pretty much stopped growing tall in the third grade, I never even *played* basketball—not even "Horse" in driveway hoops. But I also never suffered a serious sports injury. About the worst was some minor chaffing. But I am one of the millions of vicarious athletes. Oh, I, too, abhor the professional's hubris and paycheck and sense of entitlement. But I love the game, the lines, the roars, the runs, the outfits (I *do* wish baseball players still wore the old-fashioned trousers and stirrups and white hose, instead of the baggy, floppy, hide-your-spikes attire now fashionable, but, whaddya gonna do?).

I don't read Business (I figure it's none of mine). I don't read the Style section (if you doubt this, just look at how I dress). And I turn to the Food pages only for a recipe that I can sneak onto Shelly's nightstand in the hope of a tasty casserole. (Her in-basket is bulging.) Oh, and I usually thumb through the once-a-week Science pages to see if anyone has come up with a cure for baldness or talking on cell phones in coffee shops. When I have made my world-nation-state-county-village-neighborhood-street-home tour of reading and rejecting, I wind up in Opinion and Editorials. I hate the term *op-ed*. It sounds too cool, too contrived, too hip. But that's just my opinion. My Opinion and Editorials visit makes me feel civic and civilized. The columnists are attracting or repelling, but they all have a great basket of verbs and adjectives and I just like kicking the tires of those things.

Time was I had to doff my hat at the Obituaries before putting the hat back on to sit in my Sports section seat. They appeared in ... the ... *Sports* ... section. Death reports immediately preceding the fun and games? They sure lowered the joy. Like a maiden aunt who always speaks of drowning if one were to swim immediately after eating a frankfurter. Or the auto mechanic who can gloom a simple oil change into a two-thousand-dollar-catalytic-converter-check-engine-light-yer-1938-Ferblungeon-is-on-its-last-legs downer. If I am headed to the grassy fields of frolic, I don't want to lumber through a morgue just before I step under the stadium arched entry to the sun-splashed field. I need—at the very least—the interval of time required to ignore Business, Science, Fashion, Food (the *reporting*, not the *partaking*), and Automotive ... *after* paying respects to the recently departed, before I check scores and standings and the latest dope on human growth hormones.

So the obituaries are back in the main section. Sober. Solemn. Sighing. That's where they belong. And I hope that's where they'll stay. If we didn't learn anything else from Doctor Frankenstein's lab assistant, Igor, I hope we learned that graves should not be tampered with ... or moved.

Let's go, Mets.

Yogi Fisher

"No wheels at first!" the shortstop's voice echoed in the dusty air. "No wheels at first!"

I was at first, fresh from smashing a softball into left-center field—*distant* left-center field. For a gazelle-like ballplayer, such a hit would have been a double or even a triple. I huffed and puffed it into a mere one-base hit. I've always been a loper, a trotter; why, even on a good day I can manage only a brisk waddle.

And so on first I stood—flushed with contentment (and exertion) at my safe arrival, only to suffer the tactless, albeit astute, observation by the opposing shortstop of my snail-ish "wheels." Never mind, 1979 saw my return to organized, competitive sport: slow-pitch softball.

I grew up in leafy Little Valley, New York. A charming village a few miles from Lake Erie. I read my first baseball magazine there and swung my first Louisville Slugger there. The sounds of batted ball and cheering crowd hangs in the western New York air. Honest. And you can't ignore it. *I* couldn't, anyway. Baseball was my passion—I pursued it with a frenzy. Throwing. Batting. Fielding. Tagging. Sliding. Baseball is a sport of great verbs. I read every baseball magazine on the newsstand rack: I subscribed to every baseball magazine my lawn-mowing salary would allow. My schoolbooks could gather dust in a corner or keep a table leg level, but my baseball books were devoured and digested into dreams.

I'd close my eyes and imagine that stadium in the Bronx and the public-address voice: "Now batting for the Yankees, number eight, YOGI ... FISHER!" (At the time I thought "Yogi" would echo with a stadium ring better than "Ira.")

I could hear the public-address announcer telling the gathered throng that I was advancing to the plate. It's a common American-boy reverie, one from which we only slowly awake. But when adult pragmatism weaves its thread through the fabric of our senses, we revise the dreaming to admit more reasonable pursuits. Such as ... *soft*ball.

Countless games have bounded out of Abner Doubleday's creation—stickball and pimple ball; Wiffle ball and 500. There's kickball, sawball, gumball, and hotbox. But baseball's most popular offspring is softball, with some spin-offs of its own: fast-pitch, rec-pitch, modified, and slow-pitch.

As I travel and grow grayer, I am convinced of an evil that attends competition. The striving-to-win. It knocks aside the weak and the slow. When victory becomes the only goal, the sparkle and the poetry of the game are lost in the consciousness of the player. Gone is the *charm* that lured the player to begin with. What replaces that charm is a sober singlemindedness that does not allow the game player the *fun* of the game—only the cold-blooded pursuit of ... the *win*. Shudder. I have always enjoyed merely playing.

All the same, as 1979 reached March and warmed to a yellow-green glow, I succumbed to the invitation of my sleekly athletic brother-in-law, John, to join his softball team and wear the proud colors of a fine and venerable Spokane pizza parlour (I realize pizza is Italian, but I prefer the British spelling of the *parlour* where the pizza is baked). It was an easy seduction. The uniforms were cool. Not the old, hot wools of my formative years. Today the pizza people (and service-station people, drive-in restaurant people, diner people, real estate, insurance, and we'll-take-care-of-all-your-sewage-trouble people) outfit their spartan charges with the same duds as their professional baseball counterparts: double-knit uniforms, hats and shoes and mitts and gloves and understockings and overstockings and bats and balls and bases and chalk lines. Whew. Why, the uniforms alone caused this aging dreamer to murmur, "Yes, oh yes! Play ball, indeed!"

How deeply sink the memories of muscle-stretching exertion into the dim and distant chambers of the human mind. How quickly to the surface those painful memories bubble twenty-four hours after that first softball practice. My first serious exercise since I was twisting to Chubby Checker records at high school hops. Muscles that had long lain dormant, with no demand on their time or sinew, now cried to me in pained protest, "Why, after all the years you've spent reading books, listening to music; why, after all the time devoted to petting dogs and learning to operate the twenty-four-hour ATM; why are you compelled to shipwreck this flabby vessel of a body on the jagged rocks of over-the-hill sport?"

The little boy in me was asking my body to flirt with injury. I tried to allay the fears of my quaking frame with promises to gradually ease into jogging, bicycling, racquetball, toss-and-catch; to use fewer sacks for the same amount of groceries in my determination to climb to the summit of softball. But my body wouldn't listen, didn't believe that I would really engage in sensible exercise. It knew I'd only ask the best it had to offer in my dash for first base, my mighty swing, my blazing throw. My body knew. And my body groaned.

The language of softball came sharply to my ears when we put the practices behind and stepped over the foul line into the regular season. Technology has terminology. Sports has lingo. Softball's is among the dippiest. "No stick!" (Can't hit.) "No wheels!" (Can't run.) "Good eye, good eye!" (Compliment for a batter who refuses to swing at a pitch out of the strike zone; *and always uttered twice.*) "Be a hitter, be a hitter!" (Uncharacteristically subdued suggestion to a batter who neglects to swing at a pitch *in* the strike zone; *and*—sigh—*always uttered twice.*) "Good wood!" (A well-hit ball—note here that there aren't many wooden bats left in softball. Our team had none, but to shout, "Good aluminum!" or "Good magnesium!" wouldn't be softball proper. Accuracy in softball is required only when you're *throwing* one.)

It was the very presence of some terms that caused me to note poignantly the absence of other terms: "Hum 'er to me, Babe!" (Uttered in *base*ball by the catcher to the pitcher, indicating the desire for a fastball. Such a pitch in slow-pitch softball is, by definition, anachronistic and outlawed.) "Stick it in his ear!" (One of the baser admonitions of baser-ball; it asks the pitcher to deliberately throw at the batter. Ah ... the nobility of sport.) To achieve success in softball, one has to unlimber, to make contact, to motor, to hustle. If all you want to do is play, forget it.

Is there something to be said about grown men doing what grown men do on a softball team? Uniforms, equipment, and clichés aside. It is uplifting to run through the sunshine with pals. We did that as children, and such joy ought never have a time limit. There is a simple, ageless pleasure in being with folks we like—on a softball field or a picnic. Even when we can no longer hit the home run or dive to snare the line drive, we can still laugh and revel in good company.

Somewhat obscuring the above-mentioned rapture are the gritty-dusty-infield facts of softball life. After trials at a variety of positions, I was sentenced to the pitcher's mound (actually not a mound at all, just a chewed-up rectangle of rubber within a wobbly chalk circle). In slow-pitch softball, the pitcher is the game's most vulnerable participant. Slow-pitch pitching does not require talent or athleticism. Just an ability to lob the ball in a high arc toward home plate to the waiting-to-smash-it batter. That batter is all aquiver with anticipation ... eager ... no, *drooling* to unleash an angry swing at the approaching sphere. Sometimes a savage lunge ... and a miss! More often a savage lunge and a zonk that sends that "soft" ball screaming through the infield. Therefore, the pitcher—closest player to the batter, remember, and the newly batted ball—has the least amount of time to react. There are a number of options for the pitcher at this point: *catch* the ball, *deflect* the ball, *duck*, *dodge*, or *dive*. It should be noted by you, the reader (because it is damned well noted by the pitcher), that all of these options involve ... *contact ... with ... the ... ball*. In my brief career I suffered a dislocated finger, a sprained finger, a bruised thumb, a skinned elbow, black-and-blue shins, a swollen thigh (that, no kidding, carried the imprint of the ball's stitching for a week), and a disgusting yellow and purple subsurface hematoma on that thigh. (Okay. I heard the word *hematoma* on a doctor show on television.) All from batted softballs. The fellow who named the game *soft*ball was obviously never hit by one.

Understand there was fun, a camaraderie of players and their sport, way back in little-boy time. But now the boys are men and it's difficult to leave our youth behind. But leave it we must. I stepped onto the field listening for cheers and heard only laughing. I walked to the "mound" pitching for strikeouts and received only bruises. I strode to the plate swinging for homers and achieved only a few singles. And far more outs. Sport *can* be fun, *ought* to be fun. But sometimes the memory is bigger than the reality. No wheels, Mr. Shortstop? No, indeed. I hung 'em up with my mitt one golden autumn eve ... and never put 'em on again.

XVI

A Mouse and a Month of Chills

Brr Search

This morning—this chilled morning—I fired up the computer. And as I checked e-mail, Facebook, pictures of Welsh Corgis, Twitter, LinkedIn, and pictures of Welsh Corgis and deleted the computer clutter piled along the Internet curb in trash, start here I headed to the kitchen to make a cup of cinnamon tea. Well ... my right hand was freezing. My *right* hand. My *mouse* hand.

It happens on a day like this. Cold enough that the raising of the temperature by the turning of the thermostat takes a few moments. Several moments. Too damned many moments. And my mouse isn't helping. I think, actually, it is contributing to the chill. I have always been mindful of the mouse: a nice pad (with a picture of a Welsh Corgi) to rest on; it doesn't have to skate along the wooden surface of the computer table, nor need to roll over marble or slate or—*shudder*—Formica. But that mouse is ... cold. And my right hand is cold.

A furry mouse is warm. I know. I have held a furry mouse a few times. And that furry mouse is warm and cute and whiskered. A furry mouse even *looks* warm. Oh, a little creepy hanging around a box of shredded wheat in the cupboard, but certainly warm.

And I understand that "mouse" in the computer sense is a euphemism, a nickname, a *something* to identify a *something*. In the computer sense. But it sure is cold. I can pocket my left hand at the computer. But my right hand has to be out there. Mousing. And freezing. As it scoots and clicks and arrows the arrow around the screen. Geez. Freezing.

It gets me to thinking. There is likely some electronic reason for my computer mouse to maintain a cool temperature. That's why my radio has transistors and not tubes. That's why my computer has ... uh, those computer thingies inside it. Because a computer is not just "cool"; it's (I'm making air quotes here ...) *cool*. And it *must* be to continue computing. So there is some rationale for the mouse to be cool, too. Some rationale along electric lines. But all this coldness is making me even colder.

My idea? Mouse mitten. Or mouse muff. Not for my right hand, but for my mouse. It could be wool or cotton or a colored blend like my wife's socks that—by intention—don't match. And with a mouse muff or a mouse mitten there need be only one (because having to accommodate the righty and the lefty would clutter the point and even veer into politics), so the nonmatching issue is moot. I'm on to something here. And marketing notions are swirling in my mind. I'm still shivering but beginning to warm to the idea of a computer mouse muff. Yes! A mouse muff. With a crocheted picture of a Welsh Corgi.

Nice Rally

It's the voice-mail month. August. "Hello. You haven't really reached me because I am farther away from my answering machine than you are. Go ahead, leave a message after the beep, but don't expect me to get back to you before Labor Day. At the earliest. And maybe not even then." *Vacation* is the word, but vacation is less a thing away than a condition of the calendar. August is a black hole where appointments, plans, promises, and "get-back-to-ya's" go to evaporate. But this August is different.

This August is a hero and worthy of worship. Coming up big in the bottom of the ninth. At least here in New England. Our summers are lovely affairs. Dependably. Ask John Greenleaf Whittier and Emily Dickinson. And they'll speak of "the same sweet clover-smell in the breeze; / And the June sun warm / Tangles his wings of fire in the trees" and "Further in Summer than the Birds / Pathetic from the Grass – / A minor Nation celebrates / Its unobtrusive Mass." Those two poets are in the simmering center of summer. *He's* addressing bees on the death of Mistress Mary, and *she's* going on about ... bugs. The season really drags when it comes to August. Slips and slows and stops. Ask either poet and I'll bet they'd tell you that August can't be seen because we've been blinded by the July sun or that the lemonade has spent its sugar rush so we nap ahead to September. (Also ask Whittier about his middle name, "Greenleaf"—what's up with that?)

Usually August does this (or actually, does *nothing*). *August* is the Latin word for "yawn." Well, how could it be otherwise when you have to follow the vaudeville-woven-in-Beatlemania-diving-with-dolphins-delight that are June and July? Normal June is a catapult flinging bursting melons into thirsty souls. Conventional July sparkles and pops; it elbows boredom in the ribs as it burps and guffaws and smells of pickle relish. Of course, we ask why wouldn't August just shyly slip through the door or tent flap ... because no one heard it knock? Because no one saw it coming. Or cared enough to smile and utter, "Welcome." August *isn't* welcome. Well, ordinarily. Traditionally. It's just a thirty-one-day buffer to keep July from slamming into decorous and golding September. August is to summer what February is to winter. Dull. And three days longer.

But *this* August, as I say, is a hero striding into the batter's box and worthy of worship. *This* August has come bearing a wicker basket of bratwurst and birch beer. It has whooshed into the neighborhood wrapped in shimmering streamers of sunlight and stars. *This* August has saved summer by bringing it to town, to lake, to beach, to deck, to lawn, to county fair.

June lost the season series to cold temperatures that kept the covers on forlorn gas grills. And rainy, foggy, mildewey July failed to make the playoffs for the first time since before Lincoln wore a beard (remember the year called "eighteen hundred and froze-to-death"?). And good ol' August seemed poised for another losing campaign. To continue residence in the basement of beach-house regard.

But it surprised us this year by sweeping into our shivering New England all sunny and simmered and smelling of suntan oil. August brought burgers and sherbet; sandals and loud Hawaiian shirts. It came laden with Frisbees, sneakers, plaid Bermudas, buzzed haircuts, cotton dresses, droning lawnmowers, swimming-pool giggles and goggles, shortcakes, fireflies (finally)—and all riding on cicada songs.

Had it not been for *this* August *this* year, summer would have gone down in defeat by forfeiting the game, by simply not showing up. Thanks, August. And congrats. Never imagined I'd say it, but you have my vote for MVM. Most Valuable Month.

XVII

Fall . . . or What?

Autumn Is Falling

The sun is still warm. But watch your back. Beware the shade-side of your day. There is no doubt August has packed its bags and booked a train out of town. And out of summer. I sit on the front porch to throw my little dog Lily's tennis ball across the yard so she can race after it in what Frost called "sheer morning gladness at the brim." Her chasing hasn't slowed. The happy light in her dark eyes hasn't dimmed. But does Lily know August is leaving and taking summer with it?

We'll put the cover on the gas grill. And that will bring an end to frankfurter season. No more potato salad. No more shortcakes soaking with berries. Graham crackers and marshmallows and chocolate are finished getting together; they'll keep to themselves. Lemonade is drained. Tea will be heating, not icing. Ice cubes will get a rest and jam the freezer in their confusion.

Aging August is all about angles. The lake will ripple from refreshing to shivering. A swim rejects the morning and waits for afternoon. Toss-and-catch turns more urgent. The sun won't merely set, it'll slink down the evening sky to return tomorrow with a weakening, glancing ray. The shadows of the trees confirm this. They're longer along the evening lawn. Soon the leaves will change pitch in the wind wisping through them. Their song is changing from shush to rattle. September is coming with its notion of how the countryside should dress: in colors. Festive, flared, flamed. And brief. Beauty is only a season. Never a forever.

Then the leaves will leave. And the shadows on woodsy roads will change again ... to flicker like ladder rungs on the windshield of my 1938

Ferblungeon. And that very car that takes me from where I am to where I'm going is part of the sad hurry that life has become in this twenty-first century. We zoom far too swiftly. It isn't safe. It isn't savoring. We only *glimpse* the magic of an autumn day. Those fiery leaves. That sky blue. Those sunny undersided clouds. We roll up our windows against the gathering cold. We hide our legs and arms in trousers and coats.

Night is quicker to fall. Temperatures are quicker to fall. Leaves and light are quicker to fall. It's this falling of things and an emptying of things—juice tumblers, ballparks, playgrounds, soda cans, iced coffee cups, swimming pools—that cool this time of year. The bright days are still warm, still summer, but there's a chillier thread woven in the wind, in the slanting sun. And the clouds are taking on an iron grayness, as if they're holding some secret that we pretend not to know.

Yes, the leaves will leave. They'll twirl and whirl and circle and spin in the wind ... in the chilling wind. And they will fall to the ground. They'll stop on the browned grass. And there they'll rest. Like flowers at the grave of summer.

Something to Sneeze At

October. What a scamp of a month. The leaves, the colors, the hills awash and shimmering like a big bowl of Trix. The wind takes something cold from coming winter and threads it through the day. Through the crisp and starry night. October. The cider. The pumpkins. The scarecrows. The charm. And the sudden head cold. Uninvited. Unanticipated.

We never think about the head cold. When we're splashing in the August lake or belting a Wiffle ball over the hedges of June; as we're April showering or Maypoling, or trying to ice July by pouring a glass of tea, we never consider the October head cold.

Mine's here. Just as I was delighting in light from the angling sun and how it bounces from up in the treetops to down in the piney needles along the driveway, I sneezed. "Just a mild allergy," I assured myself. Then a second sneeze shattered my optimism. And a third. And a fourth. Sneezing loudly, dramatically, disconsolately. As I was luxuriating in the mosquito-emptied air, thinking about Keats sweetly celebrating Autumn with an ode, I sneezed. My teeth were jarred and my lips were loosened. Hairspray shook out of my coiffure. The sneeze caused the CD playing on my car's stereo to freeze in its tracks. Oddly, in the eighth track. I thought for a moment I'd sneezed myself back into the '70s. It was that powerful an autumn sneeze. And only the first. Followed by sneezes two, three, and four. I'd gone from a poet loving the day to a ... serial sneezer.

And then my eyes were watering. My throat began to scratch on its way to sore. My ears seemed suddenly plugged. No! My ears *were* suddenly plugged. And my forehead felt warm and diaphoretic. That means my forehead was sweating. I heard the word back in the '70s on an episode of *Emergency* with Kevin Tighe and Randolph Mantooth. They were ambulance drivers or paramedics or firemen or some kind of emergency workers (I guess they had to earn the title of the show ... *Emergency*).

Look at me. Experiencing a fever-induced delirium. From an October cold. *My* October cold. I ought to be taking joy in the changing of the leaves, the carving of a jack-o'-lantern, the shopping for little versions of cherished candy bars (a bag for the trick-or-treaters, a bag for me). I should have been focusing on baseball's inexorable march to the World Series. I ought to have been exulting in small talk carrying terms like "bowl bid," "QB sacks," and "Nittany Lions." But no. With the advent of four where-in-the-name-of-Freddy-Krueger-did-they-come-from sneezes, the season of falling leaves, cinnamon sticks, and apple picking was blown out of my consciousness and into a tissue reaching my exploding nose just in time. And I am left hallucinating about old television shows.

I continued to try to fool myself by claiming it was an allergy. Heck, I am allergic to nothing. Well, almost nothing. I don't do well with chunks of tomato in a salad or carrying stuff up to the attic. But that's really more disinclination than allergy. And now the October head cold. Not the air cold or the leaf cold or the want-a-cup-o'-hot-chocolate-to-get-rid-of-the-cold cold. No. It's the October head cold. It's here. It's hit me. And the fragrance of October is no longer the goldened smell of piling leaves, the pungence of new apples bulging in baskets, no longer the soft sweet scent of popcorn balls sitting on wax paper, cooling for Hallowe'en.

Nope. With four sneezes and memories of forty-year-old reruns, October has taken on the odor of Vicks VapoRub. Sigh and achoo.

Warm Feet

Pardon my presumption. But if a filmmaker were ever to tell my story in a movie, it might unfold this way: open with a swirling, frothing December snowstorm as the credits flutter into focus. The woodsy hills of Little Valley, Cattaraugus County, western New York. The snow would fill the screen as it piles and plugs road and drive. Cut to a dew-eyed deer seen through the falling flakes, shivering in the chill, but glad the hunters are housed and out of the storm, out of the hunt. The quieted farms and the blue shadows from pines and barns and fence posts lengthening in the dim, departing day. Children thick with snowsuits, scarves, and stocking hats slogging to the yellow-eyed windows of home. Inside, the film of my life would find cinnamon buns and ginger cookies from my mother's oven cooling on the counter. The movie moves from panorama to close-up; from slow, wide sweep to small shot. And on the screen in a rack-focus ... slowly ... dramatically (as the opening score climbs to crescendo) appears this small, unobtrusive icon: a hot water bottle.

Think of the cinematic metaphor: the one gift that always arrived way ahead of Christmas and stayed well beyond ... the hot water bottle. December waits to be the movie of me. My movie declares that December is when I break out the hot water bottle ... that pink rubber miracle.

My childhood winters were lived in a sweet little valley just a thirty-mile snowball toss from Lake Erie. And a lake-effect storm was a frequent adventure. Before Lakes Erie and Ontario were fully frozen and chilled. Those lakes were still moist and mischievous enough to feed their damp into the air to make a wind-whipped bust-out from Canada. Oh, those snows were something. And in my movie I am forever filling the squeaky hot water bottle with ... well, hot water. *Steaming* hot water. Can you see it roiling on the screen suggesting turbulence and the passing of time? *I* can. Icon.

The hot water bottle. Glorious. Giving. Unsung. A floppy comfort, the color of a porterhouse steak. Or the sunset over Elkdale. The hot water bottle. Transmitting its holiday heat at the bottom of the bed. Keeping the star-sparkled cold beyond the wall, seeping its warming into my sock-soft feet. As day and my movie slowly darken to a diminishing dot ... that—in rubbery pink letters—declares, "The End." Excuse me. My teakettle is whistling. Time to fill the bottle.

Hibernation? No, Thank You

Perhaps you are reading this in a warmer place. A sunnier place. Some neighbors took to Hawaii for last month's holidays. I didn't accompany them, wasn't asked to do so; but, had I been asked, I'd have declined. I stayed right where the shivering solstice descended. I've spent all of my winters on the frozen side of freezing. On a recent evening some friends mentioned that they'd love to hibernate winter away and wake in the budding spring. Not I. No hibernation. No tropical vacation. I wouldn't know what to do on December sand in mere shorts and a bad tan.

This is not a sporting decision. I don't ski. I don't snowboard. Nor ice-skate nor ice-fish. The closest I ever get to that last pursuit is Mrs. Paul's Fish Sticks from the super supermarket. I pay a guy to shovel and plow. Haven't fashioned a snow*man* or a snow*ball* in decades. So I can't claim to wade out into winter for any "doing." I just watch.

It snowed on New Year's Eve. I imagine winter decided that the lighted electric ball not be the only thing to drop on Times Square. Or other parts of the crystallized Northeast. All the busy-ness of preparing for the holidays gave way to a brief time of reflection. In those contemplative moments I pulled thoughts from the dim dark back of my mind. What I found were more and greater than mere resolutions. As I settle into the new month, the new year, here are the thinkings I have dusted off for thinking:

When I drop by that market, now, for groceries, I will no longer use a shopping cart. I plan to gather from the shelves only the food I am able to carry in my arms to the checkout. I'll save money. And wind up in better shape from the exercise and fewer calories.

We have an old, old pan ... baked and caked with so many casseroles over so many years that we simply cannot clean it completely. So here's what I did: on Christmas Eve, I asked Shelly to prepare a tuna casserole in that battered old pan. It filled the kitchen with the warmth of a Yule log. I took it out of the oven and carried it—steaming hot—over to the neighbors. They answered my festive, bestive Bob Cratchit knock at the door and I smiled, extending the pan. "Anybody can send a Christmas card," I caroled. "Here's a holiday greeting you can *eat*. Tuna casserole." Four days later, the family's eleven-year-old son brought the pan back. Scrubbed and spiffy ... as clean as the day it rolled out of the factory. And as he left my porch, the boy grabbed the snow shovel leaning against the railing and cleaned my sidewalk. Don't tell me there is no Santa Claus.

The season has iced the trees and mounded the snow. Winter is settling in for its un-holidayed phase. No 'nog. No carols. No kidding. December is an elf. January is a taskmaster. A harsh one. With a heart of cold. But today as I drove my automobubble along the street I noticed the sparkle of the sun on the snow. It was just a glance, but it brought back the memory of my boyhood in the lee of Lake Erie where snow would fall one day from a gray, lumped sky ... and the next day when I went out all bundled and scarved to survey what winter had wrought ... the snow sparkled like diamonds. I enjoyed the memory but saddened thinking about the speed at which we live now. Today my view of the sparkling was all too brief. When I was a lad I savored the sight ... and crunched out into it. Nice memory. And I wouldn't have it if I had been surfing in Hawaii. Or hibernating.

Bummed Out

Hitchhiking. The preferred mode of transportation for my generation in the 1960s. I hitchhiked all over the place. To and from high school. To and from cities. To and from my first job in radio—WGGO—in Salamanca, New York.

To hail a car, I employed the hold-the-fist-with-protruding-thumb-low-at-a-45-degree-angle. As opposed to the earlier-in-the-century hitchhiker who employed the right-arm-up-bent-at-the-elbow-with-thumb-vaguely-aimed-in-the-direction-hoped-to-travel approach.

After a record hop I'd hitchhike home. "Bumming a ride," we called it. Just a couple of miles, but my motto was "Better to Ride than to Stride." I even asked my grandmother to needlepoint the sentiment into a pillow. She never did. However, one Christmas she *did* give me a festively wrapped cold pizza as a gift. One of my favorite presents ever. Even today, if I don't smell a thread of pine needles woven into the fragrant fabric of pepperoni, mozzarella, and tomato sauce ... I feel a soft sadness. Pardon the digression.

One fall when I was on the high school football team, I had an autumn-into-early-winter romance with a girl named Trudy. She lived seven miles away. In Salamanca. So I depended on the kindness of licensed strangers for me to make the journey to Trudy. And back. One late Friday evening before a next-day football game (the storied Little Valley–Ellicottville rivalry), I was hitching home from an enchanted evening with Trudy ... teenagerly happy in the still-warm memory of holding Trudy's hand and sharing popcorn. I've always felt that love blooms more from popcorn than from long-stemmed roses. Perhaps that's why I haven't heard from Trudy in fifty years.

I had walked (or *floated*, to be Keatsian about it) almost to Elkdale, halfway between Salamanca and Little Valley. And it was past midnight. The wee, small dark of game day. Headlights appeared, my thumb bummed, and a shiny-finned Oldsmobile gravel-scratched to a halt on my side of the road. I responded to the driver's "Where ya goin'?" with a confident, "Little Valley, sir."

I slid into the leather sumptuousness of the idling Olds piloted by a guy who introduced himself as "Dirk." Affable, smiling, and curious about why a young fellow like me was out so late so far from home. Usually I would make up tales—and identities—in my thumbing travels. Sometimes I was heir to the Romanov throne in czarist Russia. Sometimes I was Yogi Berra's St. Louis cousin scouting ballplayers for the Yankees. On other bummed rides I was a penniless orphan, an injured Olympic skier, an apprentice stuntman on vacation from a Johnny Weissmuller *Tarzan* film. Or the grandson of a wealthy Nova Scotia mink trapper who had disinherited me when I took up the cause of animal rights and reported him to the Canadian Mounted Police, resulting in my being unceremoniously expelled from the family mansion and forced to live in a World War I surplus pup tent that leaked when it rained. Credibility never concerned me. Merely hearing myself talk was my motivation. A way to fill the miles from point A to point B. Pointlessly.

But that night in that car I was just ... me. No fiction. Just fact. I was Joey Fisher. Third-string linebacker on the Little Valley Panthers high school football team. And out past the ten p.m. curfew the night before the big game against the Ellicottville Eagles. Smiling and smug. Dirk drove me right to my door. We laughed and shook hands as I dis-Oldsmobiled and bounded up the steps into my parents' house for a little sleep before the game.

Too few and too short hours later, I slumped at my locker as I was getting into pads and cleats. Coach Bartolotti stormed up and ordered me to immediately report to his office. I did. Immediately.

"You needn't finish suiting up," he barked (causing me to think of him as Coach Bark-o-lotti). "Yer off the team!"

"Whoa ..." I whoaed. "Why?"

"Fer breakin' curfew. That fella you hitched a ride with last night? Or, actually, *early this morning.*" (Coach was keen on details.) "Dirk? He's a buddy o' mine and he called to tell me about the nice chat he had with you ... *in the middle of the night!* Way t' go, Fish. Yer finished!"

Well, I had no one to blame but me. I broke a rule. And had to face the consequence. I skulked out of the locker room and hitched a ride home. The team went on to beat Ellicottville that golden autumn afternoon. But my gridiron career was over. And it was *my* fault. But to this day ... I still grit my teeth when I ponder that Dirk turned out to be a dork.

No!vember

Hello, November. You're settling in, I see. You've been eleven months away and now you're back. Well, be quick about it. Get the place a-shivering.

Oh ho! Your wind really sounds serious. It smells of snow. And feels flung from far Manitoba. Or Buffalo. It is singling out its victims. Your wind isn't *stirring* the *leaves*; it's *shaking* the *leaf*—each little fluttering, shuddering, juddering leaf—shaking it with ominous warning that time is up. It's a stem-down, get-thee-to-the-browned-brittle-grass-and-the-sloping-meadow ... to-the-gutter sort of wind. *We're done w' ye, leaf!* Begone from your summer branch and fall! Fall! That's the season's name: "fall." It's what you do now, leaf! Fall!

Your sun is no longer bright, November. Now it's harsh. And angular. With no warmth, no lulling, no kidding. Yours is a serious sun. Joining your serious wind. Your very name is an icy reprimand. No!vember.

But do you understand that we've put away the baseball mitt? And we're sad about that? We're sad, November, at closeting the shorts and sandals and sunblock. And sad at confronting gray leafless trees, gray iron sky, gray shadows falling on your aging, graying calendar. Some folks make a brave effort at cheer. Robert Frost claims that in November, "her simple worsted gray / Is silver now with clinging mist." I admit to being somewhat comforted that M&M's are even *less* likely to melt in my hand. They're no longer summer soft. And there is a small, pleasing relief that now you're too cold for me to go jogging. As August was too hot.

I have a neighbor so weary of the winter drudgery of shoveling snow from his driveway that he bought a driveway in Florida. Not a house. Just a driveway. Not I, November, oh no! not I. I'm staying right where I am. In New England. Prepared to take your lake-effect flakes as I defiantly stomp my numbed, booted feet. I'll still listen—head up, arms folded, undaunted—for some song in the trees as your wind tunes the branches to a minor key.

On your fourth Thursday, dear month, my house will cozy to the aroma of savory stuffing, it will steam from mashed potatoes. Pumpkin pie will work a spicy miracle on my mood. A baking bird will give great good to the day. And as these sights and smells and flavors slowly load the eager moments, I'll watch a parade. A parade of airborne balloons. And I'll smile, November, at Snoopy and Bullwinkle and a Cat in a Hat. And I will radiantly beam when Santa Claus glides into view on the final float. Yes, November, *Santa Claus!* He'll dispel doubts I've harbored since January that he even exists. *Of course Santa Claus is real, November.* I'll see him on my television on your fourth Thursday. And later he'll be at a football game in Detroit. Santa doesn't exist? Nonsense. Two sightings in two cities all in one November day. Ha! Don't make me laugh, November. Santa is real. And he arrives to save the day from all the ill you'd do it.

So hello, eleventh month. We've met. I've known you for many, many years. And you don't scare me. Oh, you might crunch and crackle more than other months. Your breath may be shagged with ice as you listen to your favorite song: the hum of my furnace. But you're a phony, November. Is that cranberry sauce I see on your chin?

XVIII

The Enlightened Time of the Year

Illuminating

There's a certain Slant of light,
  Winter Afternoons—
  That oppresses, like the Heft
  Of Cathedral Tunes—

—Emily Dickinson

Ah. A certain slant of light, varying with the season. And varying in intensity from the objects—leaves and windows and eyes—through which it passes. This Thanksgiving-time-of-year light is slanting into the angle that caught and clouded the poet's mood back in 1800s Amherst, Massachusetts.

We've hit that time of year when the glow of day is more sipped than chugged. While the eastern sky lightens up earlier, too, the other end of day sinks sooner into night. So switches and rheostats are damning the dimming in quite charming ways. The vernacular of lighting design claims a goal of illuminating "any minimalist space."

Illuminating memories. Streetlamp light through summer leaves. The soft, romantic light at a high school record hop. Christmas lights. Traffic lights. And childhood Saturday mornings. Housework. The chug of the hand-wringer Maytag in the damp and mossy cellar. The rattle of wastepaper being wadded and readied for a burning in the backyard. Those days and their peculiar chores are gone, and the air and our backs are healthier for it.

I recall the slant of light on Saturday mornings. Mom's Electrolux bumping and gasping over the lumpy living room carpet. In the soundtrack of my blue-collared generation's youth one of its melodies is the drone of the vacuum cleaner ridding the weekend of dust. Or stirring it into the morning sun slanting through the window. The tiny, spinning motes sparkled and shone as they rose and wobbled and spun until finally they sank ... soft and silent. Still there in the room. But wafted over to a new nook. That old Electrolux *tried* to gather the dirt of the week and cast it out into the November cold. It succeeded with much of it. But failed with much, as well. It is why I have often thought that vacuuming sucks.

The fashionable "decorator" lights of today keep darkness at bay. By design. In style. Spilling into shrouded corners and drawing our eyes to the lights themselves. They are there—not merely for what they do—but for their style and shape and art while doing it. I like the hangey-down lights. Those that sparkle at the ends their cords. And displayed, as they are in magazines, against their black backgrounds, they remind me of nature's design: like lightning that hangs so long in the sky that it looks like you could walk up upon its jagged line. To hike along a lightning bolt until you would just melt away from care like an ice cube in a cup of coffee.

Dickinson's certain slant need not always be *op*pressive. It can be *im*pressive, too. Light lets us read and return smiles and find keys in the cushions. It shows paths through the dark, alerts us that a truck is coming, and casts a warm glow over the Thanksgiving table. It's doing its best to lighten up. Perhaps we ought to, as well. And do some Thursday-thanking.

Carved in Stone

A couple of items caught my notice in a magazine recently. The first was a panel discussion, "For the Love of Tile and Stone," coming up on February 12. February 12. That's the two hundredth anniversary of the birth of Abraham Lincoln. Panel discussions—on loving tile and stone, not on Lincoln—run from 6 to 8 p.m. Then there are the receptions following on floors 5, 7, 8, 9, and 10. That has me wondering what's happening on the *sixth* floor. Is that where you're sent if you don't love tile and stone? If you only *like* them? And—on the sixth floor—will there be shrimp?

If you attend the "Tile and Stone" event on February 12 in New York, how does that affect Coverings 2009's "Tile and Stone Expo" April 21 through 24 in Chicago? Shakespeare's 435th birthday falls on day three of the latter event. "For the Love of Tile and Stone" will consider trends and uses, while the "Tile and Stone Expo" will offer seminars. Will either mention Honest Abe or the Bard of Avon? Look at the statues honoring these two. Pretty nice use of stone, I think. Especially the memorial in Washington and the resting place at Trinity Church in Stratford, England. And with "For the Love of Tile and Stone" and "The Tile and Stone Expo" separated by only a month and a half, there is sure to be some overlap, isn't there? And when they say "expo," do they mean "expo*sition*" or "expo*sé*"? You know ... there can be a lot of dirt on stone.

I am not likely to attend either event. I am as big a fan of stone as the next guy, but my familiarity is limited to the long ago. Limited *and* long ago, but hands-on. I used to spend a bit of time skipping stones on a pond near my boyhood home. It always seemed a sort of magic: a chunk of igneous solidity that—when properly propelled—would go for a bounding ride over the bounding water until gravity and inertia asserted their powers and brought the stone to a stop and a sinking. I learned to lean at the correct angle and to fling the stone with a side-arm flick of the wrist ... a very baseball-relief-pitcher maneuver. I learned to spot potential as I stood and scanned the stones with my expert eye. The *flatter* the better. But flatness needed to exist on only one side. Roundness was nice but not mandatory; it did not need to be a disc. The stone could be jagged or square, indented or triangular. Fomenting a serious spinning was paramount. That spinning was set in motion by the wrist-flick, and it launched the heavier-than-water object on its happy hopping. Really, the most important characteristic of the stone was the one (at least) *flat* side. Spherical and lumpy all over? No. Bad. Reject.

Will the "For the Love of Tile and Stone" attendees or presenters speak of stone skipping? Or Lincoln (who had to have known about such a boyhood joy, though he was born before the birth of baseball)? And the "Tile and Stone Expo"? Will there be any mention of the creator of Falstaff (whose weight—along with everyone else's in England—is *measured* in stones)?

Forgive my presumption. As one who is not attending either event, I have no right suggesting an agenda or topic. And I am not. I'm just wondering, that's all. And who knows why the sixth floor is not available at the Architects and Designers Building on East 58th Street in Manhattan on February 12. The shrimp issue is really none of my business. I apologize for raising it. It's just that ... well, I love shrimp. And I know nothing about tiles.

Great Word(s)

Spring was not acting its age. A recent Sunday afternoon was gray-cold with a bone-soaking dampness. I sat in a high-ceilinged room of a lovely New England colonial house listening to a poet read from her new collection. The poems were lovely and tried to warm the air. I took particular delight in one line that tossed out the word "anemones." I lost the rest of the poem as I thought, "What a great word. 'Anemones.' *Anemones.* Ah-NEM-oh-neez. Great word," I thought. "Great word. 'Anemones.'" It's one of those words that starts on a slippery slope and swerves and slithers; rises and drops in the hope of a sigh of relief if its speaker speaks it without toppling or stumbling or bumbling into uninvited, disarrayed consonants and syllables. Rather like the phrase "The seething sea ceaseth and sufficeth us," *anemones* is a word more slid than spoken, more launched than uttered. "Anemones" emerging from one's epiglottis is verbally akin to racing down a ski slope or Rollerblading on a hilly cobblestone road. It's a wiggling missile. A wobbling arrow. A flower that whip-cracks at a mentioning. It zooms; it speeds; it darts and dashes. *Anemones.* Great word.

It is right up there with *haberdashery.* And *truncate.* And *egregious* (I once read a book called *I Always Look Up the Word "Egregious"*). And *refractometer.* *Anemone* is "akin" to *serendipity.* Or *proclivity.* And *argot.* *Argot* refuses a precise pronunciation. Like *bougainvillea, argot* has many pronunciations. And all of them are wrong. It's a word that simply cannot be said. And that's why it never is. It is only written. Or printed. In the *New York Times Book Review* and catalogues for 1956 middle-school fiction anthologies. When we actually *speak* about the word *argot*'s notions, we resort to *lingo* and

191

vernacular and *slang*. Not only are *they* comprehendible, but those words are fun to say. Like *Luciano Pavarotti, Tallulah Bankhead*, and *Topo Gigio*. Then there is the verb of the word *burglar: burgle*. I know, I know, there is *burglarize*. Please. That's just plain snooty and dorky ... like *parenting* or *updating* or *marginalizing. Burgle* is a hoot. The word, not the crime. What potential for expression: "The meager beadle was boggled at being burgled of his baubles, bangles, and kibble by a beetle-eating, Beatle-loving beagle." *Burgle* is drama. *Burglarize* is ostentation. And raises your insurance rate.

Our English is a river formed by the juddering creeks of Anglo-Saxon and German and French and Spanish and computerese. Oh! And baseball ("... get to first base." "Whoa! Ya threw me a curve there!" "Gee, that sure came out o' left field"). And English is a *roiling* river. It never stops widening and gushing and curving and speeding and foaming and splitting and spitting along. It's a sparkling liquid of a language. Not cooled, frozen lava. Like Latin. Or a vacuum-cleaner sales pitch.

Yep, our English is a marvelous *serendipity*. It's fun (*snorkel*). Scholarly (the aforementioned *proclivity*). Scolding (*eschew*, to which some people respond, "Gesundheit!" People who are obviously more superstitious than learned. You know ... real *larrikins*).

And then there is *oeuvre*. Right up there with *argot*. Unpronounceable. Unutterable. Unused. *Oeuvre* ought to sparkle with stringed melodies and a glistening of harps. But it's covered with cobwebs in the attics of the *hoi polloi*. Reclining beside riding breeches, yachting trophies, and service receipts for the twin Bentleys sitting winter-long on blocks in the third and fourth bays of the seven-slot garage. *Oeuvre* seeks only an accounting from *pecuniary* for company. It would be mortified to hang out with a *demotic* dude. Shudder.

And that shudder brought me back to that reading room and that poet smiling at the applause her lovely poem *elicited*. I missed the rest of her poem. I was still whizzing down a wild and watery slide on twin anemones.

Fathering and Sonning

As we neared our destination, "Suite: Judy Blue Eyes" started radiating from the radio. I was with my son Dylan, and we were running errands. He was home from college for the weekend and we were aimed at a grocery and an office supply store. And we planned to take in an afternoon movie. As we turned in to the parking lot, Crosby, Stills, and Nash were filling the car with their sweet suite. Dylan and I added our two parts to their three-part harmony as we drummed on steering wheel and dashboard. The moment was still melodious as I slipped the automobubble into a parking slot.

I broke my singing to ask if Dylan wanted to hear the rest of the song. "Sure," he answered on beat, and we returned to the tuneful task of Crosby, Stills, Nash, Fisher, and Fisher. We sounded darned good. Judy Collins would have been proud. After the last "doo doo doo doo doo! Doo doo doo doo doo!" I turned off the ignition and we headed to the store.

That was something I never did with my dad. Sharing a love for good rock-and-roll. When he and I were together, if the radio wasn't playing Tennessee Ernie Ford, it was turned off. If it was playing the Beatles ... *it was emphatically turned off.* Abruptly. Accompanied by colorful swearing.

My son Joshua and I share a passion for baseball. And Wiffle ball. We even visited the Wiffle manufacturer's Connecticut headquarters. We have played countless innings pitching and hitting and dreaming of glory. Josh's high school team won the state championship. He played first base. Shelly and I smiled.

My son Shelby was a basketball whiz and football-gifted. We still like to watch the Sunday games and munch on chips and dips and salami. Shelby really understands the intricacies of the game. And patiently explains them to me. I'm more of an expert on those chips and dips and the salami. Shelb is a splendid poet. I love to read his words. Shelly and I smile.

Daughter, Ash, eschews sports. She is literate and literary. Writing. Acting. Performing. We talk art. We love art. And Welsh Corgis. And books. One football season we conceived a weekly family football pool. Ash's picks were terrible. But her reasons for the picks dissolved us into laughing tears. Yes, Shelly and I smiled.

Shelly, Josh, Shelby, Ash, and Dylan—*and I*—love the Beatles and Bob Dylan and the Kingston Trio and Herman's Hermits and the Mamas and Papas and the Dave Clark Five. I like the Eagles better than *they* do, but they'll patiently sit through the six-minute-and-eleven-second stay at the "Hotel California." Bless them.

In the market, Dylan picked up a bag of corn chips. Blue corn chips. And checked the carbs on the label. My father and I never discussed corn chips or carbs. And certainly never *blue* corn chips. Our corn conversations were all of an on-the-cob or succotash nature. More monologue than conversation, really. Dad sure knew a lot about corn. How to plant it. How to husk it. How to boil and roast it. But actually, we talked little of corn. We mostly just ate it.

Next, Dyl and I visited the office supply store. He needed a case for his iPod, and I wanted to pick up a USB 2.0 extension cable. Another couple of things my dad and I never shopped for. We were always occupied with that corn issue.

Then it was off to the Cineplex for the movie. A thriller with Liam Neeson. Pretty exciting. And the popcorn was exquisite. I began to reminisce about popcorn. How we used to heat it in oil in a "popper" plugged into the wall, but Dylan waved me off with, "Dad. You're talking about corn. Boring." And he was right. I crunched through the previews without talking.

My dad and I only went to one movie together. A *Frankenstein* remake back in the early '60s. No Boris Karloff. No Colin Clive. No Elsa Lanchester. The deranged doctor's creation wasn't how I (and likely, *you*) have come to picture the doomed creature. It looked like the makeup artist was having a bad day. A *bad* day. The only thing monstrous about the monster *was* the makeup job. Less like he was constructed of spare parts from Igor's graveyard raids and more like he had been spattered by a Dairy Queen blender malfunction. Dad and I never attended a movie together again.

Fathering in the twenty-first century is easier than sonning in the twentieth. But I like it that both are still kind of corny.

XIX

Pondering a Couple o' Flicks

Double Indemnity

Fred MacMurray. Steve Douglas? Robbie's and Chip's and Ernie's dad from *My Three Sons?* I just watched *Double Indemnity.* I never knew what a jerk Steve Douglas was. Wow. Not his fault. It was that floozy Barbara Stanwyck. She lured him into a nefarious life. Murder. Granted, her hubby was dull and testy and impatient and rude and abrupt and balding and a fashion disaster, but he did not deserve to be dispatched—*bumped off*, as Raymond Chandler and I put it.

As I watched the film, I was thinking perhaps his bad mood was due to Barbara Stanwyck's hair. You cannot call it a hair*style*. It was a hair *abomination*. A hair *disaster*. Who was Ms. Stanwyck's stylist on the film? Lassie? Now, *I* am no looker, granted, but what was up with that 'do? Really. That had to have been the only film in which Edward G. Robinson was prettier than the leading lady. Sorry, but, the upholstery in Barbara Stanwyck's 1944 Chevy was more attractive. That was a coiffure that desperately needed coif medicine. I'm no historian, but I am betting conditioner had to have been invented after 1944. What was up with those bangs? They looked like a tunnel through the Poconos. A tunnel through *one* Pocono, to be geographical and grammatical.

And Fred MacMurray? Come on. Those heavy-lidded squinty eyes should have been checked by an optometrist before he set out from the insurance office so he could have actually *seen* Barbara Stanwyck's locks. Not exactly platinum. More like Reynolds Wrap. No wonder Fred told Barbara that his name was "Walter Neff." On some level he must have been afraid she'd try to track him down.

Okay. I am being unnecessarily unkind about Barbara Stanwyck's hair in *Double Indemnity*. I apologize. Her character was named Phyllis Deitrichson. Dietrichson. Isn't that the German word for "bad hair decade"? Really, I am sorry. I'm done with the hair comments.

Did Fred ever tell Robbie and Chip and Ernie what *really* happened to their mom? I always wondered why Edward G. Robinson never was a guest on *My Three Sons*. Now I know.

Tomorrow, and Tomorrow, and Tomorrow

I found a film on Turner Classic Movies and it caused me to ponder Orson Welles's soundstage for his 1948 production of *MacBeth*. With my basic cable, I am able to watch TCM. (An aside here: doesn't it seem that we're losing our love for words? We're resorting more and more to initials—AOL and HBO and TCM and HOK—rather than the perfectly fine words and terms they represent: America Online and Home Box Office and Turner Classic Movies.) Okay, back to point: I considered the *MacBeth* set as interior design for a home and concluded that it lacks ... uh, amenities. MacBeth's place is all rugged-lumpy-cooled-lava-looking. Drywall clearly wasn't in the budget.

There are people all over MacBeth's place. But nobody appears to be enjoying. Anything. Even that nice party MacBeth and his lady throw. The king looks like he's just seen a ghost or something. And that crown? Come on, Orson, where did you get *that*? Burger King?

The castle is bulging metamorphic rock dripping and oozing oily water. That's not indoor plumbing. That's pneumonia as wall treatment. The woeful folks can only trudge. In black-and-white plaid, which they drag through the puddles. Ick. That throne on which the troubled Scottish king sags and mopes is enough to make a fella sag and mope. Hey, Thane of Cawdor, ever hear of throw pillows? I *do* like it that the morally muddied monarch mentions something as mundane as *rhubarb*: "What rhubarb, cynne, or what purgative drug / Would scour these English hence?" (act V, scene iii, lines 56 and 57) Indelicate? To be sure. But after severed heads displayed on stakes, the stabbing of Duncan, and a wholesale dispatching of any number of foes—imagined or real—mention of purgatives is pretty tame stuff. Yeah. Rhubarb doesn't make me think of purging the English. It makes me think of pie.

For all of his soliloquizing about "tomorrow, and tomorrow, and tomorrow," MacBeth is so yesterday. MacBeth's castle is such a gloomy place that even plaid can't cheer it up. They could really use an accordion.

XX

Ah, Yuletide and the Little Valley Wind

Fa La La . . . La

Christmas music. It first affects the Christian—the *good* Christian (Saint Francis) and the *bad* Christian (me)—in a particular way. I have a dear Jewish friend who loves Christmas music, too. It does evoke a time of year as much as a spiritual pondering. It is not enough to claim the music is nostalgic. Oh, it *is* that, yes, but its reach is further into time that just our youth. Christmas music reaches back, *way back*, before me. Before you. It reaches further back than even the day on which a certain song was composed. It reaches back into time and into the human consciousness.

I am being far too general, so permit me to speak for myself. Christmas music takes me to times of dark enchantment. Velvet cold. Sentient stars. The smell of hay and pine trees. A wind slipping over snow and susurrating through leaf-lost trees. It is on such music that we ride. It is in such music that we swirl slow, warm, numbed to the world the music invites us to leave—if only to briefly, softly touch, again, a place, a force, a scene, a renewing, a receiving, a giving, a marveling, a sighing, a loving, a returning to some sweet place, some sweet remembering for which we can find no higher name ... than love.

Every year the Christmas song returns and ushers me back to the dark, bosky hills around Little Valley which I don't want to leave, so I visit them every day in my memories. I don't want to leave there and return here to the days where people hate rain and other people, stuttering, numbed, number-weighted days on the calendar; days that speed through jagged sleep. And pile in growing unremarkable piles.

Every year the music takes me to a sweet, solitary joy. But I cannot stay.

I fail to stay. Yet, go back I *do*. Go back we *all do*. This has little to do with religion. But much to do with faith. We go back to find a whiskered grandfather on his dairy farm; to a canoeing native grandmother on a Pennsylvania river; to a black-and-white dog ... barking at a kite in the sky; to a teacher who could smile and share respect. This is where the music of Christmas takes me. This is where I fail to stay.

A Christmas Gift for Wally

Ah. Wally. My dog. Our dog. Named for a lake in Michigan. Walloon Lake. But we call him "Wally." He's an energetic Welsh Corgi. Active. No, rowdy. I mean *really* rowdy. He's all over the place. Hasn't stopped zooming around for longer than a few napping hours since we brought him home from New Hampshire as a downy puppy a year and a half ago. His motto seems to be "Live noisy or die."

So, I need to get him a Christmas gift. The perfect Christmas gift. But he's a dog, you say. Yes. He's a dog. And, of course, I *know* that. But he's Wally and he's really cute and we're so happy he's in the family ... that I want to get him a nice Christmas gift. The *perfect* Christmas gift. But ... what?

It can't be demeaningly dippy doggie duds. No wiggly antennae like a giant ant's. No kerchief with prints of pheasants or buried bones. No sweater knitted in the shape of another, bigger animal. Wally's a dog. Pleased with his species, he doesn't imitate other animals. Nor need to. And he'd never tolerate four cutesy-tootsie little boots on his stumpy paws.

I was thinking of getting him the gift of monthly meat. Like they advertise in *The New Yorker*. But what if I'm not home when the meat arrives? Wally can't answer the doorbell or sign for a parcel. As with most other dogs, he can't hold a pen nor write. Meat on our New England porch in December and January might be fine. Meat on the porch in June is not meat. It's a disease.

Pinecones might be the answer. Every holiday season my wife, Shelly, puts a charming little basket in the entryway by the front door. And fills the basket with pinecones. She has done this all of our married life. I look forward to the basket of pinecones. Like wreaths and snow and the Harry Simeone Chorale, the pinecones say "Christmas" to me. As Wally headed for the door during his first yuletide season, he veered smoothly to his left to the basket and with great grace lifted a pinecone with his teeth and continued—without breaking stride—to the door and beckoning nature. I think he saw the basket as you or I see a dish of mints on the checkout counter at the diner. For *me*; not for display. Shelly was not amused.

A box of toys? Well, for Wally, we've ventured into toys. Rawhide knotted "bones," plush stuffed bunnies, an odd pair of vinyl rectangles connected by a two-foot length of fuzzy rope. He's had tennis balls, baseballs, Wiffle balls, footballs. They last for one day. And wind up shredded and all covered in dog spit. I can't return them. I can't even touch them. After all the thought and money spent on such things, it turns out that Wally prefers an empty one-gallon plastic milk jug. That makes him really happy. It's noisy enough to appeal to his hobby of property devaluing and big enough to avoid whooshing through the slats on the deck and sending milk jug and Wally tumbling to the lawn below. But how can I, in good Christmas conscience, wrap a plastic milk jug and put it under the tree for Wally? How can I do that for him when I am buying cars and stereos and boats for the rest of the family? Well, I'm not getting that stuff for the rest of the family, because I can't afford that stuff. I wonder how they'd feel about an empty one-gallon plastic milk jug. I mean one for each. Wally loves 'em.

Winter Song

Those snowflakes in *The Nutcracker* certainly dance beautifully, but it's their singing I love. Tchaikovsky bottles magic in that passage and releases it into the moon-splashed forest. The branches droop with the weight of winter. Not a weary weight. And not really a droop, either. It's more of a bow. A bough bow. Homage to a season in which snow *sings*. It wasn't until years after encountering this scene in the ballet at Lincoln Center that I wondered how it could snow so profusely ... under a full moon (which snow clouds would surely obscure).

I don't recall the winter winds of yesteryear singing in cascading harmonies as the winds do in *The Nutcracker*. But they *did* sing. My childhood house was a single-story block box that cut those winds into melodies ... groans, actually, and different from Tchaikovsky's. My father and mother had literally built the house—framed it, drywalled it. Had a little professional help with the wiring, but they did the rest themselves. I was too young to help or understand the magnitude of the enterprise. The sweat, the talent, the vivid curse at an ill-aimed hammer. The little house rose all through the summer of my fourth year; finished and ready to keep us warm by winter. And in all the winters that followed until I heard the calling world ... and left that little house.

The snow certainly danced. But not as *The Nutcracker* snow dances. My home snow piled and pounded and pillowed and plugged. *Really* plugged. Driveways, streets, roads, sidewalks. I loved it. We had a goodly share of "snow days" off from school. My brothers—Larry and Harlow—and I would sit in our pajamas in the kitchen eating toast-and-brown-sugar, listening to John "Old Bones" LaSalles on WGR Radio out of Buffalo as he read the lengthening list of delays and closings. It was joyously excruciating. And difficult. Ever try to hold and eat toast-and-brown-sugar with all your fingers on both hands ... *crossed*? Ever end up with your pajamas covered in toast crumbs and brown sugar when "Old Bones" declares, "Little Valley Central School is closed. You have the day off!"? It's happy. Sticky. But happy.

We'd bundle up, head out into the numbing air to climb up and sled down the hills of day, and slog home in twilight, blue from the cold, but still bubbling with the serendipity of unexpected holiday. Mom would brew some "cocoa" (what we now call "hot chocolate," which seems too literal, too obvious; *cocoa* was exotic for that time and that place after a morning of toast-and-brown-sugar).

Slipping into bed meant slipping between flannel sheets and under wooly spreads and quilts sewn by grandmas and aunts. And it meant the suffusing warmth from a hot water bottle (which I have celebrated in other pages). One of winter's blessings. The hot water bottle. I'd marvel at the seeping, sleepy comfort of warm feet, warm bed, and the un-Nutcracker song of the still-falling snow. My Little Valley boyhood snow moaned and ghosted as the wind carrying it sliced on the corner of the house outside my bedroom and sounded in the creaks and cracks of creeping, assertive winter.

In winter these days I still listen for that particular wind song, that evoking pitch, but rarely do I hear it in the now. I often wonder about that little house—I have driven past it a couple of times on visits to my old, loved village. It's someone else's home now, and the wind sings to strangers. But I remember. And while the song of *my* snowflakes was no ballet, it *was* beautiful, and the snow danced a beautiful dance.

Heavy Snows

"It's said that each snowflake is a little Christmas memory come back to find who lived the memory." Okay. I just made that up.

There was nothing more pleasing to me when I was a boy than a sudden winter storm. The arctic air would team up with a front over Canada, and the two would enlist huge amounts of snow over Lakes Erie and Ontario. And the whole chilling mass would slam into western New York State with enough force to make a three-star general swoon.

We lived in Little Valley—a village between tree-covered hills, a village peopled with philosophers grown accustomed down through the years to leaving home in morning sunshine and returning waist-deep in snow. The pace of the village (if a calm, quiet, pondering existence can indeed be called a pace) shifted into neutral on every Sunday in summer and in every storm in winter.

Many of the separate strands of my memory are full of these cherished storms. I never wish anyone ill or inconvenience, but a rainstorm and a snowstorm seem to allow the world to cozy up, to step more slowly through time's passageway. Precipitation, when it comes in profuse, driving rowdiness, blots out much of life's mundanity. Neon pizza signs. Political billboards. The price of Crisco and rump roast on the market marquee. Snow pelting our good earth dims to invisibility much that is ordinary and softens to near beauty everything else. Beauty and near beauty give us good memories. Snow memories.

"I'll get Dad! Don't move!" My cousin Shirley yelled to me and peered from the top of the snowbank above my head. I could see just her face, framed in a scarf and stocking cap.

I've always suffered from a congenital lack of common sense. It was during one such lapse that I decided to amuse Shirley by jumping off the snowbank—on which she now crouched—into the ice-crusted drainage ditch below (this was in the winter after the summer that I ate three squirming angleworms in another attempt to amuse Shirley). I thought it might impress her. It did. It impressed her with just how stupid I could be. I crashed through the ice and splashed soggy snow onto my lower legs. The slush instantly froze and I was a prisoner of the ditch. And my stupidity.

I recall thinking how *sad* it was going to be die in a drainage ditch in winter. I thought how *idiotic* to die in a drainage ditch in winter. But fate smiled at me from the kind face of Shirley's father—my uncle—Ted, who chuckling and gentle reached a long arm down the snowbank, grasped my outstretched woolen mitten (covered with little ice balls), and, with great effort, pulled me back to life under the gray sky. I was hustled into their house, wrapped in a thick quilt, plunked down before a glowing old woodstove, and coaxed from numbness to tingly comfort by the fire, the love of dear people, and a whiskey sling my aunt Lutie had brewed for the occasion. The light from the fire spilled out the window onto the snow and—as the vapors rose from the hot beverage—my affection for winter and for snow and for doing stupid things rekindled. My affection for drainage ditches, however, was slower to return.

It's forgetting childhood in general, and winter and Christmas in particular, that have put a "Humbug" into the adult holiday. I cannot suppress a smile when I see snowflakes beginning to sputter out of the December sky (or the *November* sky, for that matter). It's said that each snowflake is a little Christmas memory come back to find who lived the memory. I just made that up (I've always wanted to foster a legend).

One little snowflake will return to me in the coming winter from a certain Friday in 1960. A serious storm invaded the dark of early morning and piled up several inches of snow while the wind sculpted enormous drifts, closing roads and streets ... and school (I rejoiced). My father worked for the Cattaraugus County Highway Department, whose responsibility, obviously, was to keep the highways open. So winter created mixed emotions in our house. A snow-spewing storm would send me home from school and Dad back to work. I can't count the number of times he and I must have passed each other in a blizzard.

Well, this Friday, about which I write, never fully established its light. The morning was still trying to shake night out of its eyes when the sky darkened more grimly and snow began its journey to earth. So quickly, so mercilessly did the storm deal its fury—I watched delighted from my seat in seventh grade social studies—that we were on our way home in less than forty-five snow-sparkling minutes. Likewise, nature slammed the door on any frivolous weekend travel. I imagined, dreamed, projected a closed school for at least a week into the future ... and upon arriving home that Friday late morning, I settled into Dad's easy chair (he wouldn't need it until school reopened). I sighed and relaxed with a book about Tarzan and his lion, Jad-bal-ja, and relaxed for some sweet jungle reading.

The snow fell in staggering amounts. It piled so high on the outside windowsill that I couldn't even see our driveway or the mailbox or the road beyond. Inches rose to feet. I grew confident of a two-week school closure. I left Tarzan and Jad on their own in Opar when Mom sent my brothers, Larry and Harlow, and me off to bed. The snow was still squalling and falling Saturday morning (three weeks of closed school comin' right up!). I rose from bed, bundled into my outdoor adventure attire—three pairs of pants, a cotton undershirt, three flannel shirts, three pairs of socks, one pair of sneakers, arctics (with their clanky buckles), wool parka, mittens, stocking cap, and a maddeningly scratchy wool scarf ... and headed for the great, drifted outdoors: our yard. The world I had known had come to a blinding white end. The world in its place was a smooth, frothy, swirling fantasy. Two sides of our little one-story house were obscured by drifts that curved to the very roof, thirteen feet from the ground (ah! A whole month's winter vacation!).

Harlow jumped lightly from a drifted pile at the side of the road and patted the telephone wire with his gloved hand. Larry pulled out binoculars and scanned the wondrous winter for woodchucks. I sat—literally *sat*—in the middle of the road, up to my seventh-grade chest in fresh snow. Together, my brothers and I stepped over Mom's clothesline. *Over* it! And our giggle-laced conversation centered on what to do with our leisure now that we would never be returning to school.

It was early that Saturday afternoon that the snow stopped falling. By dark, the sky showed more stars than clouds. Sunday arrived in sunshine. Drifts diminished. Icicles melted. Snowplows plowed. And snow went. To the side, out of the way.

Monday morning saw us on our way ... back to school. We passed Dad on his way home. I remember worrying that when he finished breakfast and headed for his easy chair he might sit on Tarzan's lion.

That day after school, I tarried at my pal Boober's house long enough to watch him zoom his toboggan into a maple tree and smash it to splinters. I'll never forget Boober walking away, head down, toboggan rope in hand, dragging a collection of little wood chunks along Rock City Street through the snow. I tried to cheer him up by suggesting that we jump into a drainage ditch. He declined. So I jumped solo. Some people never learn. I didn't get stuck this time, but I was blue with cold when I reached my house. Mom quickly got me out of my icy clothes while Dad drew a tub full of hot water. I slid into the steamy bath and slowly felt warmth return to my mistreated limbs. As I luxuriated in the comfort and listened to Christmas music from the radio, I thought about my earlier brush with the chills ... and the hot beverage Aunt Lutie had prepared.

"Dad!" I called. "How about a whiskey sling!"

He poked his head through the bathroom door. "We're trying to cure your frostbite, not *celebrate* it."

Winter puts many memories into all those snowflakes. I'm always glad to live where the memories don't melt before they return to earth. To find the people who made them.

Christmas?

This is the best time of the year. To me. Oh, certainly, sitting under leafy shade in golden summer is sweet. Or the day that spring finally grows up and grows green is enchanting. And autumn weaving its sunlight with a mischievous cooling can seduce. But December and winter and ... Christmas ... is the best time of the year. To me. I love the air making room for the scent of an evergreen tree twinkling in the living room for a couple of weeks. I love the night dotted with lights. All the colors of all the people on earth. I love the sound of sleigh bells in a song on the radio. Or the sound of sleigh bells from ... well, sleigh bells. Cooling down, we bundle up. Putting off woe and considerations 'til "next" year so we can celebrate now. In this moment. The best time of the year. To me. Then the snow. Or the hope for snow. Shopping just enough to raise a smile, not a debt. Giving. Receiving. Singing. Sighing. Merrying. I just read a new novel, *Mr. Dickens and His Carol*. Its author, Samantha Silva, calls Christmas "the great irrepressible annual fact." Simple. Understated. To the point. Very like Dickens. If the day is holy to you, God bless. If the day is holiday to you, enjoy. If the day is just Monday, I feel sad for you. To me "the great irrepressible fact" sparkles and glows and sings and cools and warms and suggests and delivers and delights and charms. It's Christmas. Yes, a little baby born humble and preaching peace. Or it's a day off from the thrum of the twenty-first century. It's a pause in the noise and a lift in the heart. Grouches, beware. Your nonsense makes no sense on December the twenty-fifth. Sit down. Be stilled. Be calmed. Dickens noted of these sweet and chilly days, "the broad fields were so full of merry music, that the crisp air laughed to hear it." You might just find something magic to think about, to smile about, to laugh about. You, too, might just find this to be the best time of the year.

Do You Hear What I Hear?

The wind is blowing December into this day. The temperature started in the teens. It is only in the twenties now, as the ineffective sun slants and sinks and fails to be anything other than just another ornament in the holiday sky. It snowed over the weekend. I went often to the window to look at it. To smile at it. Six ... seven ... inches. But snow. Each flake a Little Valley memory coming back to find who made that memory. That's where I grew up. Little Valley, New York. And back then, back there, my thoughts are all in night. And how the dark was only dotted—never broken—by lights. Streetlight. Headlight. Christmas lights on the tree in the middle of the village. An amber glow tipping out of the living rooms along Court Street, Erie, Eagle, and Mill under the trees. Those winters sit in my soul and rise smiling to my mind. Especially near Christmas. I loved that jingling, tire-chain burbling music muffled by snow plowed and piled to the side of the streets. I loved the crunching underfoot. I loved the air sparkling in the sheer, cheek-rosy cold. I loved holding hands and holding hearts and holding happy owned moments at the skating rink behind the movie theater. Or walking out of school onto Rock City Street at the end of the day. Or seeing snow snake over Fair Oak as cars and wind refused to let it rest. Snow too dry to form a snowball, too heaped to climb, too Christmas-y to ignore.

Some choose to leave the snow. Bless you and travel safe. I'll not head south for Florida or Arizona. I'm staying here ... in the twenties, in the cold, in my Little Valley memories ... and I'll simply sigh at a sparkling, sacred, blue-shadowed snowdrift sculpted by the wind. Like the wind that is blowing December into this day.

Another Op'nin', Another Month

New Year's Eve snow. It fell like the curtain at the end of a show called "The Holidays." New Year's Day is when we walk through the lobby of the theater smiling about all we have just seen. The lights. The tree. Presents (coffee maker, socks, a robe, a CD, a book about Saint Francis). Given and received gifts: a purse, a cardigan (the sweater, not the dog), pens, pads, paper clips. It all sparkled on the December stage. Now it's time for the stage crew to clear the props and set the setting for the next production: January.

My contemplations have led to some conclusions: everyone I know is very convincing at saying, "Wow! It's perfect!" "Just what I wanted!" "Gee! Wonderful!" "How did you know?" which inexorably leads to, "Did you save the receipt?" We give slippers every year because after a couple of weeks with a drying, browning pine tree in the living room you really don't want to walk around in socks. Eggnog isn't a beverage; it's some mysterious revenge. The song "I'll Be Home for Christmas" wistfully asks, "Please have snow and mistletoe and presents on the tree." Who puts presents *on* the tree? Accuracy would be better served and poetic meter *pre*served with "presents 'neath the tree." And reviewing the holiday bills has made me realize that precious few things in Freeport, Maine, are free.

A period of my post-holiday meditating came in a room where I was waiting for an appointment. There was a sign posted on one of the doors: "This door must be kept closed at all times." Whoa. (In my mind I actually formed the word *whoa*.) What's the purpose? If it can never be opened, it's no longer a door. It's a wall. With a knob.

Well, here's the overture. Shh. The curtain is just going up on January.

XXI

Giants

Broadcasting and Bigness

Giants. We all know them. We all know giants. And they are many in our lucky lives. Two of my many giants touched my life for over forty years. You never know when you will meet a giant. You never know how that giant will give your life a lift, a lilt, never-to-be-forgot. Giants take life and fill it with light, they make it glow. Laughter is always bubbling up or waiting nearby. In the company of giants tears are understood, never need explaining. Giants conjure such words as *greatness* and *grace*. Giants have nothing whatever to do with size. *Physical* size. A giant's size is a hugeness of heart, of intellect, of wisdom.

I have met many giants. You also have met many. The gift—of the giant—is that she or he be recognized, be acknowledged by us who meet them. The giant must be recognized, acknowledged. And embraced.

Of the many giants I have been blessed to know, I write here in depth of two. Heaton and Clooney. And a love the three of us shared. The love of a microphone. A microphone is more than a sender of sound. It is a door to a place called imagination. It lifts the curtain on the stage in the theater of the ear and mind. The microphone was the love Chuck Heaton, Nick Clooney, and I shared. Chuck's love was a microphone in the state of Washington. Nick's was in Kentucky, and mine hung from the studio ceiling at a little radio station in western New York.

As life unfolded and the miles multiplied and led me places I never planned nor anticipated, I encountered the talents of those two giants. I listened to that talent and—smiling—I stole from it. They were older than I. At a time when most people were. Now few people and fewer giants are older than I, but when Chuck and Nick and I shared a common love, they were giants. To hear, to delight to, to embrace with the mind. And the heart.

Chuck coaxed laughter out of every day he lived. Laughter and a lack of pretense, an empty-of-nonsense brightness that kept KHQ Radio singing and speaking and news-ing with a lofty level of that thing nowadays they call "professionalism." To use the argot of those radio days, they fostered and inspired "a tight board," no "dead air," and "riding good levels." Chuck had been a disc jockey (as Nick and I had) when the term meant someone who played records on the radio and "announced" between the songs.

Chuck and his late wife Peggy (a nurse) had a sweet family: sons Rick, Ryan, and Regan, who were loved and grew to loving adulthood. After Peggy's death, Chuck found love with Julie. The Heatons are a family of giants. Wisely, the KHQ management appointed Chuck program director at the radio station—Q-59 (AM 590). And in that capacity he hired me as a staff announcer in the autumn of 1970. I was planning to stay in the Pacific Northwest for about three months before returning to WGGO in Salamanca, New York (where my microphone love affair had been kindled six years before and interrupted by a four-year military hitch).

So, as that Spokane December approached I mentioned to Chuck that my time at Q-59 was drawing to an end. He challenged my plans and gently suggested that I at least think about staying. So I did. For the next ten years. One of the sweetest decades life gave to me. A giant decade. In the company and sunniness of a giant named Heaton.

There was a sports announcer in town named Dick Wright. He was a play-by-play man with Herb Hunter (Spokane Indians baseball, Pacific Coast League affiliate of the Dodgers). He also broadcast the Washington State B-Basketball Tournament and went on to become the radio voice of the Gonzaga University Bulldogs. And, more important, he introduced me to his daughter, Michele (whom I lovingly nicknamed "Shelly"). And with whom I fell I love. And in 1972 Shelly and I married. Chuck and Ed Sharman and Harv Clark and Cal Fankhauser (fellow radio buddies—and giants in my life—at KHQ) were groomsmen on that happy, happy day.

Chuck wasn't a boss. He was a big brother. And not all that big. Actually

5 feet, 6 inches. A fellow disc jockey—Barry Watkins—dubbed him "the gnome." And Chuck smiled at the designation. He could receive as well as give. Because of my notable waistline (waste-land, as I called it), I was "the round man."

Chuck was impish and perceptive. He knew what new record would be a hit and what new record could go directly from turntable to trash can. We relied completely on his judgment. I could never pick a hit. Chuck always could.

Then, broadcasting being broadcasting, I was offered a job in television (I usually claim the offer was tendered because I was so tall, slim, and handsome ... then I pause for laughter). I had started working both radio and television at KHQ when a television station in Cincinnati invited me to meet with its bosses. I was attracted by the offer because I am an easterner and I longed for the green-leafy charms on the other side of the Mississippi River.

You need to know, at this juncture, that I had stopped traveling by airplane in April of 1970. I had spent four years in the Air Force, and its jets and propeller craft had failed to seduce me. Well, in fact, they dramatically exacerbated my acrophobia and dread. So to get from Spokane, Washington, to Cincinnati, Ohio, I needed to engage in a two-day crawl by train to Chicago and an overnight bus ride to Cincinnati. It was worth it. Because the long, long journey led me to the second giant of these musings. My circuitous—and prolonged—travels provided this second giant with a funny tale that he often told, and embellished each time he told it. I laughed with each embellishment.

Nick Clooney. Giant. He fell in love with his microphone at a little radio station in Maysville, Kentucky, in the early 1950s. He embraced and thrived in a career of radio disc jockey, newsman, master of ceremonies for events. (Serving in that role in 1959, he met his dear Nina at a beauty pageant. She a contestant and Nick the emcee of the event.)

As it happens, Nick actually *is* tall, slim, and handsome. Unlike me. He is also talented, affable, witty, and smart (*really* smart), and dresses with great style. With *panache*. I never had occasion to apply that word to myself. I've always told Nick that I suspect he even sleeps in a suit and tie. He has never denied it. So television was a natural next chapter in Nick's microphone love affair.

So, on that steaming Cincinnati summer day (all the Cincinnati summer days are steaming) when that Greyhound bus dropped me off, Nick was the managing editor and main anchor for WKRC, Channel 12's *Eyewitness News*. He was already a legend. And a giant. A giant who welcomed me to his team of giants.

Allow me to address the obvious here: Nick hails from a family of giants. His sisters Betty and Rosemary Clooney were superstar recording artists and found film fame. Nina has produced and hosted television programs. Their daughter, Ada, is a dear and endearing and intelligent writer and mother. And their son, George, has left his large, legendary footprint in television and Hollywood. And the entire Clooney family has bettered our world by championing the oppressed and giving voice to the voiceless through their philanthropic and physical and progressive presence in Africa, Europe, and America. The Clooneys have faced the maw of fascism and ripped out many of its cruelest fangs. The family is a blessing in our world. The family is a giant.

Fame is an odd thing. It comes in small and large doses. I mean it reaches far or stays closer to home. And fame is something that rises from newspapers and glows from televisions and shines from motion-picture screens. Sometimes fame rides in on a singing voice. Or an acting scene. Or words of the day's events uttered into a microphone and a studio camera. We put a great deal of stock in fame. But fame is an odd thing. If it is your goal, you will likely never know it. But if fun and the honest pursuing of a worthy, entertaining life is your goal, there is a chance that fame will come along for the ride.

Back to Nick and me. We sat elbow to elbow at the news desk for three magic years. Along with Denny Janson (who every day—every ... single ... day—dissolved us in tears of laughter), sports anchor, Cincinnati native. And giant. Nick delivered the news. With class and conscience, intellect and urbanity. I reported the weather. And wrote and delivered frequent essays on various topics. Denny shared scores and interviews and insights. And he never wore socks.

We lived three years in Cincinnati. One day an agent—Conrad Shadlen, a giant—called from New York City and paved my way to WABC Television. And then to WNBC. And ultimately to WCBS and the CBS network. New York. The Big Apple. A couple of small roles in film. A five-year frequent appearing in *The Fantasticks*, the long-running, legendary Harvey Schmidt and Tom Jones musical at the Sullivan Street Playhouse in Greenwich Village. A giant of a play.

We gather every couple of years in Cincinnati. To remember and hug; to tell stories and laugh. Then we motor forty-five miles up Route 52 to a ferryboat float across the Ohio River to Kentucky ... *to Augusta.* Hometown of Nick and Nina and Ada and George. We dine at the General Store and the Pub and the Beehive. We sit and we talk the rambling talk of friends who are more a family late into the humid Kentucky night. We look up to see magic things: Fireflies. Shuddering tree leaves. How the river dances with the moon. And talk. Oh, how we talk. Stories bubble and fizz. Sleep finally comes, only to abruptly end as we wake to the dawn foghorns of ambling barges. There's dew on the grass and flower petals. And there is our talk. Always our talk. Even the trees seem to smile as they lean and eavesdrop on this loving chattering.

It's a seven-hundred-mile trek from Connecticut to southern Ohio. Along interstates bordered by trees and rising hills, dotted with travel lanes, cars and semis, and the occasional grumbling motorcycle. There are gas stations, fast food enticements, and shreds of truck tires on the shoulders. Connecticut waves into New York where the wide Hudson River reminds you that there is something worth crossing. Hilly green Pennsylvania flattens at the Ohio line. The sky widens. The clouds expand and sigh. There are thunderstorms to zoom under and through. Always a thunderstorm. Or three. And rain over the Midwest is a serious rain. It's more than mere sheets. It's bedspreads, grayed pillows ... and loud like a scolding uncle. But rain is good. It gives us deciduous glory.

As I said at the start of these musings, the giants in our lives are many. And like the acknowledgment page in a book, I note some of those many.

225

Sharman, Clark, Watkins, Miller, Mell, Schram, Giorgi, Rogers, Blair, Herriges, Howard, Baker, Cottam, Stimson, Shook(s), Vigdorth, Dixon, Magnus, Gasper-Keith, Reeb, Traynor, Andrews, Braun, Burrows, Dixon, Hildenbrandt, Ciccarone, Ain, Elder, Langford, Rose, Herbert, Bolton, Soller(s), Hurdlebrink, Tenhunfeld, Angeline, Dickaut, Finelli, Wise, Seimers, Koch, Hart, Maher, Ryle, Herbert, Grimsby, Beutel, Snyder, Tong, Orsillo, Hsu, Slattery, Philbin, Anastos, Roker, many, many giant Smiths, Mitchell, Goldfarb, Lillis, Geiser, Kessler, Walton, Powers, Blume, Lindner, Dee, Simpson, Jones, Pennolino, Johnson, Carroll, Guida, Statsky, Palmer, Hart, Koch, Wright, Cook, Tost, Bernstein, Miller, Chenowith, Martin, Blankenship.

This collecting of names is woefully incomplete. Some are missing or blurred in my aging mind. But you are here in joy and gratitude in my glowing heart. You are here. You are giants. And *giant* is just another word for *blessing*.

About the Author

Ira Joe Fisher grew up in the western New York village of Little Valley. Its hills and trees and winters and summers – and people – live in his heart and writing. He has spent his life in broadcasting – radio and television – and in performing. He regularly appeared in the long-running musical *The Fantasticks* from 1995 to 2000. He was "Henry VIII" in the musical *The Prince and the Pauper* at New York City's Lambs Theatre. Ira also performed with Skitch Henderson and the *New York Pops* at Connecticut's Ives Center. He took the role of "Monsignor Buckley" in *The Garden of Dromore* at the New York University Hot Ink Festival. Ira had a role in the film "California Girls" and "Try to Remember: The Fantasticks" and in the ABC daytime drama "Loving." He appeared for many years on CBS Television's *Early Show*. He teaches poetry and literature at the University of Connecticut and at Mercy College in Dobbs Ferry, New York. Ira and his wife, Shelly, live in Connecticut.

You can connect with me on:

🌐 http://www.irajoefisher.com

🐦 https://twitter.com/irajoefisher

Also by Ira Joe Fisher

Remembering Rew

Some Holy Weight in the Village Air

Songs From an Earlier Century

The Creek at the End of the Lawns

CPSIA information can be obtained
at www.ICGtesting.com
Printed in the USA
FSHW011044171020
74818FS